INSIGHT GUIDES

DUBAI &
ABU DHABI

smart guide

D DUBAI
16 – 17

APA PUBLICATIONS **L**

Part of the Langenscheidt Publishing Group

ternational Airport

Contents

▲ Beaches and Brunch:
Recover from the night's excesses with the famous Dubai or Abu Dhabi brunch, followed by beach lazing.

▶ Big Attractions keep the malls and hotels full of tourists and locals.

◀ Shop-'Til-You-Drop:
Traditional souks, blinding bling and giant malls: Dubai's still the king of consumerism.

▲ Messing About on the Water:
Drift down Dubai's creek or Abu Dhabi's corniche on a traditional dhow or *abra*.

▲ A Day at the Races: See the camels or horses careering around the race tracks and witness genuine Bedouin culture. **◀ Islamic Insights:** take a tour of the newly completed, vast and extraordinary Great Mosque in Abu Dhabi. 3

Dubai and Abu Dhabi

Ever since the disastrous demise of the pearl diving industry in the 1930s, the United Arab Emirates has been hard at work cultivating a newer type of gem – tourism: one that's almost as valuable, but even more marketable. From little more than specks of sand, the cities of Dubai and Abu Dhabi have grown pearl-like into two of the fastest-developing, most dazzling and dynamic cities on Earth.

Dubai and Abu Dhabi Facts and Figures

Area of the Emirate of Dubai: **3,885 sq km (1,500 sq miles)**
Population of UAE in 2010: **8.26 million**
Peak temperature in June–September: **48°C (118°F)**
Low temperature in January: **15°C (59°F)**
Area of the Dubai Desert Conservation Reserve (DDCR): **225 sq km (87 sq miles)**
Inhabitants of the DDCR: **57 plant, 120 bird and 43 mammal and reptile species**
Length of the Dubai Metro system: **76km (47 miles)**
Height of the Burj Khalifa: **828 metres (2,716.5 ft)**
Area of Dubai Mall: **12 million sq ft**
Number of retail outlets in the Dubai Mall: **over 1,000**
Length of the Dubai Mall Aquarium: **50 metres**
Number of marine inhabitants in the Dubai Mall Aquarium: **33,000**
Volume of water in the Dubai Fountain: **22,000 gallons**

Dubai's Shooting Star

Dubai, the city of 1001 lights, is the world's first celebrity town. An exotic outpost in the desert less than 20 years ago, the city has clawed its way up to A-list celebrity status through a touch of talent carefully honed, clever management, overriding ambition and all-out self-promotion. Glamorous, flash and fast, the city excites adulation and admiration, contempt and revulsion in equal measure. But love it or loathe it, Dubai makes an impression. Considering the speed at which it has developed from fishing port to centre of finance, Dubai's greatest achievement might be how it has coped with rapid change and its newfound fame.

Many visitors get their first glimpse of the city from the plane. The famous Burj Khalifa, the tallest building on Earth, is so high –

stretching not far off a kilometre into the sky – that it must don its own flashing light to alert approaching planes to its presence. Boasting some of the world's most iconic modern buildings, designed by some of the world's greatest modern architects, Dubai can claim the world's most startling skyline.

Building a Dreamworld

Home to a fifth of the Earth's cranes, the city has sprouted in all directions: outwards, upwards, and even downwards. Sand, sky and now sea are subjugated for the greater good of *Project Dubai* – a government-driven

Below: brighty coloured, traditional dress contrasts with Dubai's sleek skyline.

Above: luxury flats in Dubai Marina.

mission which has transformed Dubai into a world centre of finance, trade and tourism. Hydropolis was to become the world's first underwater hotel; the gargantuan palm projects were to see hundreds of islands fashioned from the sand and the sea which, when completed, would have doubled Dubai's land area in its entirety. Some projects have been resounding successes; Palm Jumeira's visitors 'walk on water' and the views from the top of Burj Khalifa are similar to that only seen from planes before. Dubai has had to rein in some of its ambitious plans and cancelled projects outnumber those completed. This does not deter Dubai; its quest to inspire with audacious innovation goes on, despite the dip in world economies.

Abu Dhabi, the Capital City

Abu Dhabi, Dubai's shyer, more conservative and less boisterous brother, meanwhile busies itself as the Emirates' capital. Though less glam-and-glitz than Dubai, it still boasts great beaches, world-class hotels and fine dining. Carving out its own niche as a kind of cultural capital, it will soon have its very own Guggenheim and Louvre, billed to contain among the world's greatest art treasures.

Topping the Tourism Tables

Long packaging the old tourism chestnuts of sun, sand and shopping, Dubai, and to a lesser degree Abu Dhabi have sold themselves spectacularly, particularly to northern Europeans seeking winter sun. Adding to the equation world-class dining, fabulous nightlife, and the hosting of the world's top sporting events, the cities' aim is to outdo any destination on Earth.

Not to be outdone elsewhere, you can drift, Venice-like, down canals, and swim with dolphins. Like a cell turned mutant, Dubai is now seeking to outdo even itself: it's planning a new, new-tallest-building-in-the-world.

Digging for the Past

Though both cities are criticised for their loss of traditional culture and history, you don't have to dig too deep to find it. Lose yourself in the warren of alleyways and souks in the old quarters of Bur Dubai and Deira, or the dhow construction yards of Abu Dhabi. A trip to the camel races juxtaposes ancient tradition with modern luxury like no other: robots sit atop careering camels pursued by *dishdasha*-decked owners in their latest Lexus 4WD.

Love them or loathe them, the cities truly account for all tastes... *Bismillah* – enjoy.

5

Dubai: Deira

'Deira' popularly describes the sub-districts lying immediately north of the Creek. A visit here is a must. Not just for some of Dubai's most colourful encounters, perusing the old souks and cruising the Creek, but for anyone remotely interested in understanding the city. It was here that some of the first *barasti* (mud and palm-frond) settlements sprouted, that Dubai began to carve its career as a trading centre, and that people from all across the Earth began to settle. It's also here that you get to glimpse Dubai's fascinating underbelly: old rather than new; East versus West; past versus future and labourer versus lord.

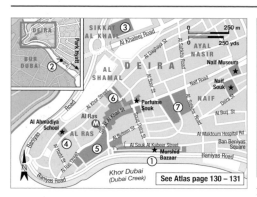

Above: Deira Fish Market.

CREEK

Around the mouth of the Creek mushroomed Dubai's earliest settlements, and up and down its water came the commerce that would make the city rich.

Following the Creek on either side is the **Corniche** ①, a gorgeous place for a walk in the early morning or evening. Look out for the restored **wind-towers** lining the bank of Bur Dubai, and some of the city's most iconic modern buildings lining those of Deira.

At the **Dhow Wharfage** ② you can watch goods being unloaded from these ancient ocean-going vessels just as they have for

centuries, only now the cargo is more likely to consist of air-conditioning systems, plasma TVs and Dualit toasters. **The Terrace** in the **Park Hyatt** is a great spot to rest legs, replenish liquids and see the Creek from above.
SEE ALSO ARCHITECTURE, P.27; BARS AND CAFÉS, P.31; DHOWS, P.49; HOTELS, P.70

DEIRA FISH MARKET ③

Well worth a wander, particularly in the early morning when the night's catch has been brought in, is the **Deira Fish Market**, lying due north of Al Ahmadiya Street. Apart from the wooden crates containing fish of all shapes, sizes and colours,

there's a little museum paying tribute to this once vital industry. It showcases the 350 fish species of the Gulf, the city's fishing past, and the tools and trade of its fishermen.
SEE ALSO FOOD AND DRINK, P.64

AL AHMADIYA STREET

Lying on Al Ahmadiya Street is **Heritage House** ④, a former pearl merchant's house dating from around 1890. Now restored, it's a fine example of a traditional Emirati courtyard house.

Directly behind lies **Al Ahmadiya School**. Founded in 1912 by a philanthropic pearl merchant, it was the emirate's first school. Rooms, containing

Left: floating along Dubai's Creek.

indelible impression (though you may have to dodge deftly the fake watch and handbag hawkers). Some of the shop windows are positively blinding, and at night, the place appears almost Aladdin-esque.

Consisting of more conventional shops, the **Perfume Souk**, close to the Gold Souk, is interesting mainly for the bags of *bakhoor* (incense) and *oudh* (aloes wood) that are much loved locally. Once more valuable than gold, the best of both these aromatics can still fetch exorbitant prices.

A little further east, the semi-covered **Covered Souk** ⑦ is Dubai's oldest. It's less interesting for its contents (largely Tupperware and household knick-knacks) than for its multicultural customers and slice-of-Dubai-life. Seek out the tiny cafés serving multicultural cups of tea.
SEE ALSO SHOPPING, P.115, 117

A **boat ride on the Creek** is the perfect way to appreciate this historic waterway. If you haven't got the time or means for a dhow cruise, do what the locals have been doing since the city began and hop on an *abra* (traditional water taxi) that connects one side of the Creek with the other (and sidestep the terrible street traffic in the process), or try chartering your own *abra* if your bargaining skills make a match for those of the boatmen (a decent cruise up down the Creek should cost around Dh50). *See also Transport, p.126.*

---

school memorabilia, lead off a starkly simple, arcaded courtyard. There's a short but informative film about the *Development of Education*. Among the subjects taught were jurisprudence, Arabic calligraphy, astronomy – and pearl diving. Look out for

the original and beautiful carved teak entrance doors.

SOUKS

You may well smell the nearby **Spice Souk** ⑤ before you stumble across it. One of the last remnants of the covered Old Souk of Deira, it's no match for some Middle Eastern spice markets, but is well worth a visit. Some of the vendors speak English and can provide fascinating insights into the traditional remedies still favoured locally over modern medicine, including hibiscus-infused tea for regulating unruly blood pressure.

Even if bling's not normally your thing, a trip to the **Gold Souk** ⑥ is not to be missed. One of the largest gold markets in the world, a stroll through the dazzling arcades leaves an

---

Employed for millennia in Arabia, the uses of *bakhoor* (incense) range from medicinal (to help heal after childbirth), cosmetic (to perfume clothes and hair seductively), and ceremonial (at weddings and to welcome guests). Long used medicinally as an effective treatment against swelling, the properties of incense were recently revealed in Germany. The aromatic smoke was found to contain 'Boswellic acids' that did indeed show signs of alleviating chronic inflammatory diseases, including rheumatoid arthritis.

Bur Dubai

'Bur Dubai' is the name given to the mishmash of districts cradling the southern side of the Creek. Comprising Dubai's oldest area, it is home to some of the city's historical highlights, including several intriguing museums and some energetic art galleries. It is also home to Dubai's vast Asian community, who have made it very much their own. Here perhaps more than anywhere, visitors can track down the one thing the city's accused of losing, but can never buy: its soul. A wander through the alleyways of old Dubai without guidebook, map, intent or purpose, particularly at night, provides many with their most memorable city moment.

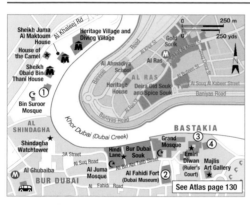

See Atlas page 130

Above: Bur Dubai Souk.

AL SHINDAGHA ROAD

Lying just off Al Shindagha Road is a series of historical buildings that house exhibitions. The **Shindagha Watchtower** is one of Dubai's rare historical buildings, which once served to alert the city's citizens to impending peril, including pirates that once plagued the waters of the Gulf.

The neighbouring **Heritage Village** and **Diving Village** style themselves as living museums. You can see craftsmen at work, including women basketweavers and potters, as well as traditional singing, dancing and storytelling.

The newlyopened **House of the Camel**, close to the road, provides a surprisingly interesting introduction to this bedrock of Bedouin culture. Rooms contain informative films on the animal; don't miss the one on camel racing if you can't make it to the races.

Nearby is the **Sheikh Saaed Al Maktoum House** ①. Built in 1896, it's a traditional courtyard house, and served as the home of several Dubai rulers until 1958. Exhibits include colonial-era documents, but the highlight for most are some exceedingly evocative – and revealing – black and white photographs of old Dubai.

Next door, the **Sheikh Juma Al Maktoum House** provides an excellent introduction to the traditional architecture of Dubai and nearby towns.

SEE ALSO CHILDREN, P.40; MUSEUMS AND GALLERIES, P.84

ALI BIN ABI TALIB STREET

Near or just off Ali Bin Abi Talib Street are a number of major attractions. The impressive 18th-century Al Fahidi fort houses the **Dubai Museum** ②. Providing a useful overview of the city's history, culture and development, the collection includes some traditional pearling boats and a *barasti* (traditional mud and palm-frond house). In the basement, a series of alarmingly lifelike dioramas (complete with sound effects)

Left: gathering for prayer at the Grand Mosque.

only conservation area.

The area's name comes from the traders who migrated from the Bastak area in southern Iraq in the 1900s. Lured here by tax-free concessions, the wealthy pearl traders and merchants brought their distinct building style with them: the traditional wind-tower house. A wander around the cool and atmospheric alleyways of the area is a pleasant way to pass a morning or afternoon.

Contained inside the quarter are some interesting art galleries, including the **Majlis Gallery** and the **XVA Gallery** ④. Even diehard non-culture vultures may opt to visit. Both provide the opportunity to see inside beautifully restored **wind-tower houses**. In the courtyard of the XVA, cold drinks, snacks or meal, are served in the pretty courtyard, and you can feel at first hand the efficacy of the ancient cooling system.

SEE ALSO ARCHITECTURE, P.27; BARS AND CAFÉS, P.31; HOTELS, P.71; MUSEUMS AND GALLERIES, P.84

Dating from 1787, the **Al Fahidi** fort served as the city's first major sea defence and for a time also accommodated Dubai's rulers.

---

include a traditional souk, and pearl diving and Bedouin life pastiches.

Near the museum is the **Grand Mosque**, which is less than a dozen years old, though built in the style of its 1900 predecessor.

Lying at the heart of the area popularly known as 'Little India' is **Hindi Lane**. Doing a roaring trade with Dubai's huge Indian community (42 percent of the population) who come to purchase religious paraphernalia with which to adorn the nearby Hindi and Sikh temples, it's particularly colourful at night.

Though less famous than the souks of its northerly neighbour, the **Bur Dubai**

Souk is still well worth exploring, and the traditional arcade that houses it is more completely restored. At its centre lies the so-called Textile Souk, with reams of fabric leaking from shop fronts that glitter and dazzle (particularly at night) almost as much as Deira's Gold Souk. Don't miss the chance to explore the surrounding alleyways, and seek out the stunning views of the Creek from the nearby wharves.

SEE ALSO CHILDREN, P.39; MUSEUMS AND GALLERIES, P.84

BASTAKIA ③

Challenging two cultural stereotypes in one, Bastakia demonstrates that Dubai *does* have some history and *is* concerned about keeping it. Snatched from the jaws of the bulldozers and currently under renovation, Bastakia is being turned into a pedestrian-

---

Bastakia's **wind-tower houses** were traditionally built of coral and limestone, and decorated with gypsum. All rooms gave onto a central courtyard, preventing sunlight from entering. The towers *(barjeel)* themselves acted as an early form of air-conditioning system, and, with the quarter's houses constructed in close proximity to one another in order to keep out the sun, the buildings were perfectly adapted to the Creek climate in contrast to the air-con-dependent 'greenhouses' of the city today. *See also Architecture, p.27.*

Jumeira

Comprising a stretch of coastline around 15km (9 miles) long, the area popularly known as Jumeira stretches over several sub-districts from just south of Port Rashid and Bur Dubai, all the way down to the Dubai Marina area. Once it was the site of a solitary fishing village; nowadays, according to the city's 'Jumeira Janes', the well-heeled European expats who make their home here, it's the only place to reside, shop and sunbathe. With its long line of whitewashed villas, luxury spas and cosmetic clinics, it looks more Beverly Hills than UAE. For the visitor, its fine beaches are the main attraction, plus a sprinkling of art galleries and two of the city's most iconic hotels.

JUMEIRA MOSQUE

Lying at the northern end of Jumeira Road, the **Jumeira Mosque** ① has been dubbed Dubai's most beautiful. Though visitors familiar with the Islamic architecture of other Middle Eastern countries (and now the new Sheikh Zayed Grand Mosque in Abu Dhabi) may be disappointed, the locals hold it dear (and even give it pride of place on the Dh500 note).

More significant is the fact that it's the only Dubai mosque open to non-Muslims. The Sheikh Mohammed Centre for Cultural Understanding hosts visits six days a week (www.cultures.ae). Architecturally, the interior's not a must-see, so if you can't make a tour, a drive-by at night when the building is dramatically lit makes a good second.

SAFA PARK

Running parallel to Jumeira Road is Al Wasl Road (one of Jumeira's main roads), not least because it provides the principal entrance to one of Dubai's best parks. For a few dirhams this manicured park offers a slice of everyday city life: people having picnics under the

trees, runners on the jogging track and families in numerous playgrounds. In the cooler months, it's an antidote to the malls and bling.

JUMEIRA OPEN BEACH

Situated next to Dubai Marine Beach Resort & Spa is one of Dubai's most popular public beaches, the **Jumeira Open Beach** (also called 'Russian Beach'). It draws expats of all nationalities and can get crowded at weekends. Favoured also for its fine strip of white sand is **Umm Suqeim Beach**, which lies not far from **Jumeirah Beach Hotel**.

A popular paying beach club is the **Jumeira Beach Park** ②, which as its name suggests is half-park, half-beach, with good facilities including parasol and sun-lounger hire.

Lying around 500m/yds due east of the Jumeirah

Left: Burj Al Arab.

BURJ AL ARAB

Though recently challenged by the new Burj-on-the-block, the Burj Khalifa, the **Burj Al Arab** ④ remains for the time being Dubai's number one architectural icon, as recognisable as Paris's Eiffel Tower or London's Tower of London.

Famously proclaiming itself 'the world's only seven-star hotel', entry for non-guests is only possible by dining at one of their restaurants, having a pricey drink at the **Skyview Bar**, or taking afternoon tea at **Sahn Eddar**. But it's worth every penny, if only to gawp at the astonishing architectural creation that the Burj unquestionably is, and take in the spectacular views from the building.
SEE ALSO BARS AND CAFÉS, P.33; HOTELS, P.71

MADINAT JUMEIRAH ⑤

This luxurious and opulent complex is so vast (combining several luxury hotels and villas with a large shopping mall and entertainment centre including theatre) that Venetian-style waterways (complete with *abra*-styled gondolas) help transport hotel and restaurant visitors around the place. The *1,001 Nights*-styled mall contains some excellent restaurants, cafés and bars.
SEE ALSO HOTELS, P.74; SHOPPING, P.116; THEATRE, DANCE, MUSIC, LITERATURE AND FILM P.122

Majlis, meaning 'place of sitting' in Arabic describes a room in a private home used to entertain family and guests. Traditionally it was here that Arab kings and rulers would hear the people's problems, grievances and complaints – the famous Arab style of democracy, and today, many Islamic countries still name their legislative assemblies *majlis*.

Beach Park behind a large, fenced enclosure is the **Jumeira Archaeological Site**. It is not yet open to the public although special permits can be obtained from the Dubai Museum. The remains – just the foundations of buildings are visible – belie the importance of the site. Once an important caravan stop on an ancient trade route linking modern-day Oman with Iraq, artefacts excavated from the site date from the 3rd to 7th centuries AD,

some of which are now displayed in the Dubai Museum *(see p.84)*.

Lying just over 1km (⅔ mile) to the south of the Jumeira Beach Park around 100m/yds east of Jumeira Road is the **Majlis Ghorfat Um Al Sheef** ③, (Sat–Thur 8.30am–8.30pm, Fri 2.30pm–8.30pm) Its main interest – besides its rarity value as one of the very few remaining historical buildings in the area – is as a traditional two-storey building, constructed (in 1955) of coral rock, gypsum and palm fronds (forming the roof). Inside, the traditional *majlis* is worth a look, and outside the gardens have been laid out to demonstrate the traditional Arabian *falaj* irrigation method in which well water is conducted around a grid of channels.
SEE ALSO HOTELS, P.72

If you've never visited a mosque before then here's your chance. **Tours of the Jumeira Mosque** take place at 9.45am daily from Saturday to Thursday.

Sheikh Zayed Road and Downtown Dubai

Sheikh Zayed Road can seem intimidating from ground level with its multi-lanes of traffic hemmed in by skyscrapers. Since the 1990s, the area has increasingly eclipsed the Creek as the city's new business district and for many, its dramatic skyline and expat haunts are still the definitive Dubai. Downtown Dubai serves in part as a residential area with its multitude of sand-coloured apartments on the doorstep of some of Dubai's best shopping, designer hotels and the trendy eateries of Souk al Bahar.

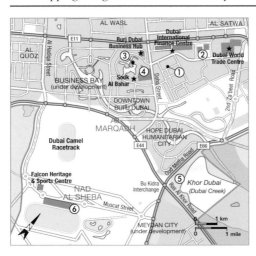

Above: Sheikh Zayed Road.

DUBAI INTERNATIONAL FINANCIAL CENTRE

Just east of Sheikh Zayed Road is the ever-developing **DIFC** (Dubai International Financial Centre). It's where high flyers forget their desert surroundings and chat over coffee before hurrying into cool, cosmopolitan offices. Dubai's equivalent of Wall Street, it's also one of the city's famous free trade zones (operating independently of the Municipality). Look out for the 'Gate', designed like a triumphal arch and housing Dubai's stock exchange.

Now also home to one of Dubai's major new art areas, a number of dynamic galleries can be found here which exhibit changing exhibitions of Middle Eastern and international art, including **Art-space** ① and **Cuadro**. In the evening, city slickers head straight for the multitude of fashionable bars and restaurants.
SEE ALSO MUSEUMS AND GALLERIES, P.85, 86

EMIRATES TOWERS

Known as Dubai's 'twin towers' and one of the city's new architectural icons are the **Emirates Towers** ②. The taller tower is not open to the public; the smaller twin contains the **Jumeirah Emirates Towers Hotel**, as well as its own mini mall, the **Boulevard**.

A good spot for some post-retail relaxation is **Vu's Bar** on the 51st floor, itself something of an institution on the after-hours scene. A visit is worthwhile just for its spectacular views.
SEE ALSO BARS AND CAFÉS, P.34; HOTELS, P.75; SHOPPING, P.117

BURJ KHALIFA

The long-awaited, much-vaunted **Burj Khalifa** ③ is now one of Dubai's greatest attractions. It opened

Left: Emirates Towers.

ping. In fact, the Orientalist interior is surprisingly atmospheric and its shops contain a decent selection of good-quality Middle Eastern exports. It also contains some of the city's finest restaurants made finer by the fact many have terraces which overlook the Dubai Fountains. Every evening, the floodlit fountains burst into action accompanied by epic music which adds to the drama.

SEE ALSO SHOPPING, P.116

RAS AL KHOR WILDLIFE SANCTUARY ⑤

The city's sole nature reserve, **Ras Al Khor Wildlife Sanctuary**, lies around 15km (10 miles) south of the city in the Creek's basin. During the cooler winter months, it attracts birds (mainly waders, shore birds and the odd bird of prey) in their thousands, including hundreds of Greater flamingos. Three hides have been established from where you can observe the birds and identify them with the help of useful information panels.

SEE ALSO CHILDREN, P.43;
ENVIRONMENT, P.50

MEYDAN

The new **Grandstand** and **Racecourse** at **Meydan** ⑥ opened in 2010, comprising a 67 million square-foot racecourse, a futuristic-looking grandstand with a capacity for 60,000, and a five-star trackside hotel in which almost every room has a grandstand view of the racetrack.

SEE ALSO RACING, P.98, 99

Until recently, the Al Quoz area was an industrial area comprised of warehouses, factories and industrial plants. But the quarter has begun to attract artists and now forms one of Dubai's major art centres. Within walking distance of each other are the **Third Line**, **Gallery Isabelle Van Den Eynde** and the **Courtyard**. The first two are known for their patronage of Middle Eastern artists and the last consists of several galleries, some craft shops and a café, set around a peaceful cobbled courtyard. *See also Museums and Galleries, p.86, 87.*

in 2010 and offers visitors not just the usual boutiques, bars and restaurants, but a nightclub, luxury spa, Armani-decorated interior and a boutique hotel, plus an observation deck on level 124, served by the world's fastest elevator.

On 17 January 2009, the tower topped out at 818m (2,684ft), officially becoming the tallest free-standing structure in the world. But the building comprises only one part of the US$20-billion development dubbed **Downtown Burj Dubai**.

With over 1,200 shops covering an area the size of 50 football pitches, the **Dubai Mall** ④ comfortably stole the largest-mall-in-Dubai crown. Keen to keep shoppers from rival malls, extras include an Olympic-sized ice rink, an aquarium boasting the largest acrylic panel in the world, the largest gold souk in the world, the largest cinema complex in Dubai, and an entire waterfall cascading down one interior wall.

The **Souk Al Bahar** next door seems like *1,001 Nights*-gone-shop-

13

Dubai Marina and the Palm

The area commonly called 'Dubai Marina' (or 'New Dubai') stretches from just south of Madinat Jumeirah all the way to the Jebel Ali Port and Industrial Area. Dubai Marina proper lies geographically and metaphorically at the epicentre of this area. Currently under construction is a whole new city; high-rise apartment and office blocks surround a yacht marina. The Palm is now a neighbourhood in its own right. Hundreds of villas and apartments offer sea views proving that even an artificial beachfront sells property as well as being a lure for tourists who want to stay on the Gulf's edge.

complex is kept at a steady -2°C (28°F), you can ski, toboggan, make snowmen and chuck snowballs. It's even got its own Black Run.

Found also within the walls of the mall is the **Dubai Community Theatre & Arts Centre**, which regularly stages musicals, plays, concerts, opera, children's shows and many other arts-related events. Besides two theatres, there's also an exhibition space, library and café.
SEE ALSO CHILDREN, P.41; THEATRE, DANCE, MUSIC, LITERATURE AND FILM P.122

MALL OF THE EMIRATES

Until recently the largest shopping centre in Dubai, the **Mall of the Emirates** ① contains some 500 shops, including its very own branch of Harvey Nichols, London's favourite designer store.

Keen to keep its customers entertained – and contained – it's also home to a food court, a cinema where the top tickets buy leather-upholstered armchairs and an on-call waiter, and myriad marvels for the kids including a decent-

sized 'Magic Planet'.

The Mall also houses one of Dubai's most popular – and polemic – attractions, **Ski Dubai Snow Park**. Outside, the temperature may top 40°C (104°F), but inside, where the whole

PALM JUMEIRA

Around 2km (1 mile) due north of the Marina lies the causeway that connects the mainland with the first of the 'famous four' palm projects, **Palm Jumeira**. The other palm projects at

Right: Palm Jumeira.

Left: Mall of the Emirates.

place for a walk, particularly in the evening, when the developments are lit like giant lanterns.

Marina Walk (or The Walk), the attractive boulevard at the base of the Dubai Marina Towers (built in the late 1990s and one of the first developments in the area), is the site of a selection of good cafés, bars and restaurants with great views across the Marina. Look out also for the Jumeirah Beach Residence, with no fewer than 40 towers headed skywards. Almost a town within a city, JBR (as it's known), contains thousands of apartments and it's a popular place to live for hard-working singletons who want to be close to the action and the beach.

If you've always fancied smoking a *shisha* (water pipe), here's your chance. Various restaurants can oblige, including the much-loved **Chandelier**.

Marina Market ③, with a reputation for supporting local arts and crafts, sells craftwork at its weekend market during the winter.

Deira and Jebel Ali are currently on hold.

Atlantis The Palm ②, the island's flagship resort with its prime position at the

When it was completed in 2005, the **Ibn Battuta Mall** became the biggest single-floor shopping centre on Earth. Named (and themed) after Ibn Battuta, dubbed the 'Middle East's Marco Polo', who spent nearly 30 years of his life travelling the world in the 14th century, each of the six sections represents one of the countries he visited. Each 'country' contains its own special feature, such as a giant junk in 'China', Ibn on an elephant in 'India', a vast, blue-tiled dome in 'Iran', and a mock mud-brick *qasr* (fortress) in 'Tunisia'. If you can – or want to – visit only one mall in Dubai, this isn't a bad choice. Among its other features are an IMAX screen and some high-quality cafés and restaurants.

very 'top' of the tree opened in 2009, at a cost of US$1.5 billion (the launch party alone cost US$20 million). It grabbed headlines not just for its excessive opening but its fallout with environmental groups who disagreed with its famous aquarium featuring a Whale shark, the Earth's largest living fish, that by nature is pelagic. There was a lot of pressure to release the animal back into its natural habitat including a 'Save Sammy' campaign (supporters had named the shark Sammy). One day Sammy disappeared and it was never made clear if the Whale shark was released or died in captivity.

DUBAI MARINA

With stunning views of the high-rises, yachts and the Arabian Gulf, the Marina makes a very pleasant

Donald Trump may have pulled out of his plans to build a hotel on the Palm but it didn't mean other hotel chains lost interest. Some of the biggest names in the hotel world have taken up residence on the Palm. The location lends itself to exclusive large-scale luxury with the promise of a private and pristine beach. Some of the most well-known include Fairmont the Palm, the Jumeirah Zabeel Saray, designed to look like the Palaces of Ottoman, and the romantic One&Only The Palm.

Around Dubai

A trip out of town is a good of way regaining some perspective after spending some time in Dubai. With traditional culture and history aplenty, a whole host of excellent activities on offer and a slower, more sedate pace of life, you can escape the carefully manufactured, tightly managed, Western-cast world of Dubai Inc., along with its haste, hurtling speed and hedonism. Many attractions lie just a short distance from the city and make good day trips. Car hire is easy, or you can charter a taxi or join one of the organised tours. You may even get to know the local Emiratis, and experience at first hand their famously warm welcome and hospitality.

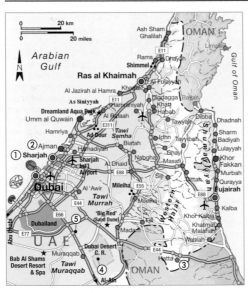

NORTHERN EMIRATES

Lying northeast of Dubai are four emirates that make up the UAE's seven. More modest in size, stature and means, they're less developed and retain something of their original identity and culture.

Once wealthier and more powerful than Dubai, **Sharjah** ① has hung on tenaciously to its history and culture. The town boasts an impressive number of museums, galleries and cultural centres, as well as well-preserved souks famous for gold, silver rugs and carpets. The town also offers excellent outdoor eating and some lovely walks along its creek and cornice.

Ajman ②, lying just north of Sharjah, is the Emirates' smallest member. It boasts beautiful, clean beaches and some good resorts (offering good water sports) and restaurants. It's also famous as a centre for **dhow** construction.

Along the coast, **Umm Al Quwain** is a popular stop for its **Dreamland Aqua Park**, the biggest waterpark in the Middle East. The town is known for its seafood, in particular crabs, which you can catch and cook yourself.

Bordering Oman is **Ras Al Khaimah**. The backdrop of the Hajar Mountains makes it a picturesque place. Drives through diverse and dramatic landscapes are its main attraction. It also boasts good museums, ancient archaeological sites and excellent restaurants.

EAST COAST

Considered a UAE highlight, the East Coast offers a bit of everything. With its attractive setting and good facilities, **Fujairah** makes a good base from which to explore the area. It's also one of the few places you can see watchtowers and old fortresses, some more than 200 years old.

Just south of Fujairah is **Khor Khalba**, famous for its mangrove forests, the most northerly in the world.

Left and below: Ajman village; off-roading near Dubai.

Hajar Mountains, a number of impressive historical buildings and a well-designed museum. Some natural attractions lie around the town, including the Hatta pools.

THE DESERT

If you've never 'done' the desert before, a trip here is a must. Apart from offering stunning sandy scenery, it can provide a great insight into what the region must have been like, pre-Dubai and pre-oil.

A tour can be worthwhile, especially if you learn something about Bedouin culture along the way. But choose carefully. The alternative is to stay at one of two desert resorts lying less than an hour outside the city.

The **Bab al-Shams Desert Resort & Spa** is a slightly Disney version: kitsch and comfortable, wonderfully indulgent and great fun.

The eco-minded **Al Maha Desert Resort & Spa** ④, ranks as one of the most exclusive resorts in the Middle East. Set within the Dubai Desert Conservation Reserve, it takes its environment and its guests seriously. Activities include falconry, horse riding and camel trekking, wildlife spotting and desert drives.

SEE ALSO DESERT EXCURSIONS, P.44–7

Lying a few kilometres off the E66 that runs southeast of Dubai, the **Al Lisailli Camel Race Track** ⑤ is the perfect antidote to Dubai: colourful, chaotic, noisy and unpredictable, it's also deeply rooted in the Bedouin past. For anyone interested in witnessing living, breathing, evolving traditional culture, here's the place. It's a sight you'll never forget. *See also Racing, p.101.*

Attracting a huge amount and diversity of animal, bird and plant life this extraordinary habitat is perhaps best explored by a canoe trip.

If you're keen to see the UAE's underwater attractions, the fishing village of **Dibba** on the far northeast coast is considered a good spot.

Various local operators offer diving and snorkelling trips offshore and to nearby **islands**.

Dibba beach is also a pleasant place to camp.

Further south, not far from Khor Fakkan, is the fishing village of **Badiyah**, home to what is believed to be the oldest mosque in the Emirates. The original building dates to the 15th or 16th centuries and forms part of an area that archaeologists believe has been inhabited since the 4th millennium BC.

HATTA ③

Lying close to the Oman border, **Hatta** is one of the most popular day-trip destinations from Dubai. The town boasts an attractive setting at the foot of the

17

Abu Dhabi: Corniche

'The Corniche' refers to the coastal strip stretching from the beginning of the Breakwater in the west to the start of the Al Meena area in the east. Sheikh Rashid Bin Saeed Al Maktoum Street, which runs north–south, forms an unofficial boundary between the areas known as East and West Corniche. In many ways, Abu Dhabi's Corniche epitomises the city: malls, five-star hotels, pretty parks and verdant lawns. Throw in a couple of reminders of the city's past in the form of the souks, the dhows and the Heritage Village, and there's your city, contrasting old mainly with new. For most visitors, the five-star shopping, hotels and dining assure a pleasant stay.

AL MEENA

Al Meena (the name given to the northeastern tip of Abu Dhabi island) is home to **Port Zayed**, the city's port, and some of its famous free zones. It's worth a walk (though photos are not allowed).

At the Al Meena **Fish Souk** ①, slippery creatures of all shapes, sizes and colours can be seen. It's most interesting when the night's catch returns (around 4.30am), though the market usually remains open all day. To the north, the **Al Meena Fruit & Vegetable Souk** also warrants a wander for its amazing variety of fruit and veg imported from far afield.

To the west is the **Iranian Souk**. It's worth a

glance for its impressive collection of kitsch (mainly household), though unless a dhow has recently returned from Iran, it can look rather depleted.

East of the Fish Souk is the **Carpet Souk**. At first sight it's not promising, but take a step inside and you'll soon dig out the more authentic and better-quality Kashmiri, Afghan and Iranian imports.

At the **Dhow Harbour** ② stretching out west of the fish market, you can see recently returned dhows unloading cargo of all types, just as they've done for centuries. Early evening is the best time, when they come in. Some of the captains can spin a yarn or two if you can find one who

speaks English.

The harbour is also where dhow dinner cruises are offered, including on board the **Al Dhafra Restaurant** ③, whose nightly cruises along the Corniche are popular among expats and their visitors. The Shuja yacht belonging to **Le Royal Méridien Abu Dhabi**, just off the Corniche Road (East) also offers popular cruises, particular for those after a romantic dinner. Board at 8pm Mon–Sat.
SEE ALSO DHOWS, P.49; FOOD AND DRINK, P.65; HOTELS, P.80; SHOPPING, P.114

EAST CORNICHE

The Corniche, the strip of paved paths, pavilions and picnic-areas lining the

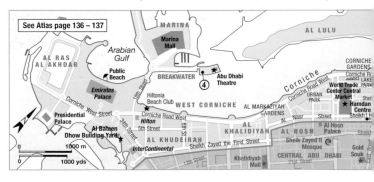

Left: modern Abu Dhabi.

reclaimed land and gives great views east towards the city. The **Marina Mall**, currently the city's largest and glitziest is here, and contains the spanking-new **Snow World**, Abu Dhabi's equivalent (not to be out-done) of Ski Dubai. Rising above it is the new **Tiara** restaurant, which, situated 126m (328ft) from the ground, boasts spectacular, revolving views of the city.

Lying close to the enor-mous flagpole is the **Her-itage Village** ④. Aiming to provide an insight into the region's history, traditions and culture, exhibits are wide-ranging and well done, and include a recre-ated *barasti* (traditional hut), a Bedouin camp, and an arcade of workshops containing local craftsmen demonstrating traditional arts and crafts. It's also a good place to pick up a last-minute souvenir.

SEE ALSO MUSEUMS AND GALLERIES, P.88; RESTAURANTS, P.111; SHOPPING, P.117

water, is Abu Dhabi's heart. It's to here that locals invari-ably gravitate to picnic, play cards, meet friends, court or take exercise.

Slicing across the city from northeast to south-west and loosely marking the boundaries of the Cor-niche is **Hamdan Bin Mohamed Street** (popu-larly known as 'Hamdan Street'), a favourite street for shopping among expats, including the popu-lar **Hamdan Centre**, and providing an antidote to the sometimes sterile environs of the malls.

Here too you can find the old **Central Souk**. It recently re-opened after undergoing a major facelift and has been transformed into a chic new quarter with markets, shops and offices.

WEST CORNICHE

Abu Dhabians are very proud of their parks and gardens, which defy the environment they live in and drink up vast amounts of desalinated water, but are immaculately tended. One of the best is **Al Marka-ziyah Gardens**, where you can rest, enjoy a bite of lunch or bring a book.

BREAKWATER

Connected by a short causeway to the Corniche, the Breakwater comprises

Beckoning at the far western end of the Corniche is Abu Dhabi's answer to the Burj Al Arab in Dubai, the **Emirates Palace**. It was designed to accommodate the city's visiting VIPs, and was touted as the most expensive hotel ever built when it opened in 2005. You can visit its glittering grandeur on your way to dine, drink or take tea at the hotel's presti-gious bars and restaurants. Look out for the gilded lobby, the Swarovski crystal chande-liers, the petrified palm trees lining the corridors, and the dazzling white sand on the beach (specially imported from Algeria). *See also Hotels, p.79.*

Central and South Abu Dhabi

Stretching from just south of the Corniche to the bottom of Abu Dhabi island, the central and southern areas encompass the business district, the historic heart, the old airport, most of the city's malls and unquestionably the most spectacular monument in Abu Dhabi's history: the Grand Mosque. With attractions ranging from serious shopping to Islamic architecture, from concerts and old boats to horse racing, the area has enough to keep most visitors occupied for a day or two.

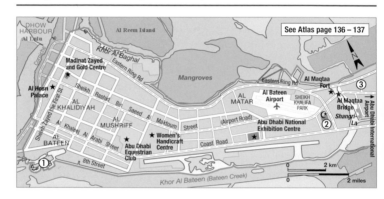

MADINAT ZAYED

Offering around 400 outlets, the **Madinat Zayed** is considered a must-shop for those after a bargain. Slightly more unusual are the little perfume shops selling local aromatics, including *oudh* and *bakhoor,* aloe wood and incense. For millennia, these once highly valuable products have been used in the region for ceremonial and cosmetic purposes.

Many visitors head here for just one thing: the **Gold Centre**. Though it's not as atmospheric as Dubai's Gold Souk, the dazzling window displays make an impressive sight. Photography is not allowed.

SEE ALSO SHOPPING, P.117

AL MUSHRIFF

Primarily a residential area, Al Mushriff is home nevertheless to a couple of places that merit a visit.

The **Women's Handicraft Centre**, at the end of Karama Street, is a government-funded initiative with two aims: to help local women learn a trade and make a living, and to preserve the traditional art and crafts of the region.

The complex includes an exhibition hall containing displays of traditional costumes and jewellery.

For a terrific night out, and an escape from the cosseted confines of the city's hotels and restaurants, head for the **Abu Dhabi Equestrian Club**.

Race meetings take place every Sunday during the winter, non-members are welcome and there's no entrance fee.

SEE ALSO RACING, P.99

DHOW BUILDING YARD

Located on a small island in the Khor Bateen (Bateen Creek), and connected by a causeway to the mainland, is the **Dhow Building Yard** ①. Dhows still form an important part of the region's economy, importing and exporting goods across the Persian Gulf, the Red Sea and even the Arabian Sea to countries as far afield as Pakistan. Here, traditional boat makers employ almost the same designs,

Left: Sheikh Zayed Grand Mosque.

boasts the world's largest handmade Persian carpet and the world's largest chandelier and can accommodate 41,000 worshippers. The daily tour is not to be missed and runs from 9.45am until 11am. It is advisable to dress appropriately and ladies may borrow an *abaya* from inside the mosque grounds.

As you cross the **Al Maqtaa Bridge** that connects Abu Dhabi island to the rest of the emirate, look out for the tiny **Al Maqtaa 'fort'**, a 200-year-old watchtower. On the opposite bank is the **Hosn Al Maqtaa**, dating from the same period. Both buildings are closed pending restoration.

Facing the island is the award-winning five-star, the **Shangri-La**. It has its own waterways served by *abras*, an upmarket souk, the **Qaryat Al Beri** ③, and stunning views across the water to the Grand Mosque.

SEE ALSO HOTELS, P.81

tools, materials and techniques as they have done for centuries.
SEE ALSO DHOWS, P.49

MANGROVES
The natural mangrove forests of the eastern side of the city are a world away from the hustle and bustle and a surprising eco-tourism asset. It's possible to explore them by kayak on a guided tour from the Noukhada Adven-

ture Company (www. noukhada.ae). Quietly paddling along the many little islands, looking out for wildlife and gaining a distinctive view of Abu Dhabi's skyline is a highlight for those in the know.

SOUTH ABU DHABI
With its huge white domes soaring celestially on the horizon, the **Sheikh Zayed Grand Mosque** ② is astonishing even from afar. Up close, its scale, conception and statistics are staggering. Costing US$2.2 billion, it was the brainchild of the late president, Sheikh Zayed, who insisted in overseeing almost every detail. He summoned the world's best designers, craftsmen and material from all over.

The fourth largest mosque in the world, it

Left: a young equestrian.

The **Al Hosn Palace** (White Palace) marks the historic heart of the city and is Abu Dhabi's oldest building. Built in 1793, the year the city was established, it served for a time as the official residence of the ruling Al Nayhan family. Though not open to the public, the fort is worth a look from the outside. It is one of the few buildings to conjure up old Abu Dhabi. Standing in stark contrast to the gleaming high-rises that dwarf it, it's also a dramatic reminder of the break neck speed of the city's development.

21

Around Abu Dhabi

Y ou don't have to travel far to escape the high-rises, congestion and commotion of Abu Dhabi. Within an hour – depending on the traffic! – you can be snorkelling off an island, watching camels career down racetracks, or standing atop terracotta-coloured sand dunes. A little further afield is the oasis town of Al Ain, which, with its forts and millennia-old date-cultivation techniques, refutes the snipe that Abu Dhabi has no history or culture. Surrounding villages could come straight out of the city's Heritage Centre, except that they're the real McCoy. As for the famous Empty Quarter, at over 1,000km (620 miles) long it puts even Abu Dhabi into perspective.

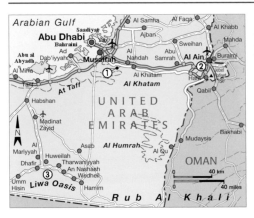

Putting the city's abundant water resources to good use, Sheikh Zayed famously 'greened' Al Ain using seven natural oases, giving rise to the town's name, 'the Garden City'. Far less developed than either Abu Dhabi or Dubai (though several megaprojects will soon start to change this), Al Ain feels more organic, more human in scale, more sure of its identity – and more Emirati. It's also laid-back and welcoming, and with its shaded date-palm oases and lush, cool gardens, it's a lovely place to explore.

Other attractions include the **Al Ain Museum**, detailing the city's heritage and history, the famous **Camel Market** (the last of its kind in the Emirates), the very animated **Livestock Souk**, and the **Al Ain Oasis** with its ancient *falaj* (irrigation) system.

AL WATHBA CAMEL RACETRACK

Lying 46km (29 miles) from Abu Dhabi on the Al Ain road is the **Al Wathba Camel Racetrack** ①. The 10km (6-mile) track attracts competitors from all across the region during the racing season (Oct–end Apr), and is well worth a visit if you come during the winter. It's a colourful, noisy and atmospheric affair in which you can witness a true vestige of Bedouin culture in full action. Old contrasts with new like perhaps nowhere else: camels ridden by robots chased by traditionally dressed owners in air-conditioned cars. Entrance is free and there's no particular dress code.

SEE ALSO RACING, P.101

AL AIN

Situated 149km (93 miles) due east of Abu Dhabi on the border with Oman is the capital of the emirate's eastern region, **Al Ain** ②. Once a key staging post on the caravan route that linked the modern-day UAE and the Arabian Gulf to Oman, the town brims with historical buildings and sites, with no fewer than 18 forts, including the 175-year-old **Al Nayhan** fort, where the emirate's late president was born.

AL AIN ENVIRONS

Around Al Ain lie various other attractions, including **Buraimi** (forming the Omani side of the oasis), with its colourful souk (look out for the antique silver *khanjars*, the classic Omani curved dagger),

Left: Yas Marina Circuit.

dunes that are the main attraction. Popular among expats, the oasis has attracted the inevitable luxury accommodation, but some tour operators now travel here if you haven't got your own vehicle.

YAS ISLAND

Half an hour from Abu Dhabi a vast playground has been created. Primarily known for its **Yas Marina Circuit**, Formula One fans can now watch racing there in the most futuristic and state-of-the-art surroundings. There are numerous hotels and the theme park, Ferrari World. The **Yas Marina and Yacht Club** (as well as being a 143 berth marina and yachting centre) is also a venue for concerts which has seen some of the biggest names, including Beyoncé and Madonna, entertain Abu Dhabi.

and nearby, a number of forts including **Al Khandaq**, thought to date to over 400 years old.

Lying around 25km (15 miles) due south of Al Ain and dominating the plain for miles around is the 1,180m (3,870ft) limestone mountain of Jebel Hafeet. A drive to the top is worthwhile just for the stunning views of the Empty Quarter and oases below. There's a car park and a small café.

LIWA OASIS

The famous Rub Al Khali, known in English as the **Empty Quarter**, is the largest sea of sand on Earth. A trip to the **Liwa Oasis** ③, which lies around five hours' drive due south of Abu Dhabi on the edge of the Rub Al Khali, makes a memorable journey.

The drive takes in some

spectacular scenery (including some of the largest dunes in the emirate), gives a real sense of pre-oil Arabia (the one the British explorer Wilfred Thesiger so memorably described in his book *Arabian Sands*), and also retraces history: it was from the Liwa Oasis and the Bani Yas tribe that Abu Dhabi's rulers descended.

Though Liwa is no picture-postcard oasis, it's the

Some visitors leave Abu Dhabi with no idea that it's an island. In fact it's one of another 200 that lie scattered off its shores. Most are flat, featureless and uninhabited, but after the high-rises, crowds and traffic of the city, a trip around them may provide the perfect antidote. Off some of the island's reefs, there's quite good snorkelling, and Humpbacked dolphins are sometimes spotted. Occasionally, from March to July, migrating whales pass through the waters. A couple of islands can be visited privately or through tour operators, including Bahraini Island, lying around 40 minutes by boat from Abu Dhabi island, which offers sandy beaches and a wildlife sanctuary.

Right: Liwa Oasis.

A–Z

In the following section the cities' attractions and services are organised by theme, under alphabetical headings. Items that link to another theme are cross-referenced. All sights that are plotted on the atlas section at the end of the book are given a page number and grid reference.

Architecture

Dubai and Abu Dhabi boast some of the world's most iconic buildings designed by some of the world's leading architects. But like a city stockbroker who is only as good as his last deal, Dubai and Abu Dhabi see themselves as only as good as their last building. New projects are announced daily, and the municipality mapmakers scramble to keep up. But for the international architects brought here, the cities are a dream. Handed a *carte blanche* in terms of design, materials, and above all, budget, they can – and do – realise their wildest fantasies.

TRADITIONAL ARCHITECTURE

Using locally available building materials that included coral rock, gypsum and date palm timber, there were essentially two types of house used for the two different seasons: the *masayf* for summer, distinct for its use of wind-towers *(see right)*, and the *mashait*, a courtyard house used in winter. Usually houses were built very close to one another in order to keep the streets shaded and cool. The narrow network of lanes also acted as little wind tunnels, cooling the quarters still further. A good example of this type of town construction can be seen in Dubai's Bastakia quarter in Bur Dubai.

BARASTI HOUSES

Well suited to the torrid climate of the Gulf was the *barasti* house. Simply constructed of poles made from date-palm trunks interwoven with palm fronds, the materials withstood the heat and moisture well and

Above: traditional architecture features fine details.

the construction allowed air and sea breezes to circulate. Once, in the pre-oil days, *barasti* houses would have been seen right across the Gulf. Today, good examples of *barasti* house can be seen at the **Dubai Museum**, and the **Heritage Village** in Abu Dhabi.
SEE ALSO MUSEUMS AND GALLERIES, P.84, 88

COURTYARD HOUSES

The classic design of domestic Islamic architecture is the courtyard house. Essentially rooms are built around a central courtyard.

Facing inwards, out of the sun's rays and exposed to the air circulating naturally by convection between the four walls of the courtyard, rooms were kept cool. The inward-facing design also allowed for a high degree of privacy, an important aspect of domestic Arab architecture even today. Good examples of courtyard houses can be seen at **Heritage House** in Dubai, and the layout of one at the **Heritage Village** in Abu Dhabi.
SEE ALSO MUSEUMS AND GALLERIES, P.88

Left: downtown Dubai, the Burj Khalifa and Dubai Fountain.

domed *haram* or prayer hall. At the centre of the courtyard, mosques traditionally had a fountain, the water from which was used in the obligatory pre-prayer ablutions. Today, rows of taps are more common.

The first minaret – another distinctive feature of mosque design – appeared long after Mohammed's death. Prior to that, the muezzin (prayer caller) stood on a roof in order to summon the citizens.

A fifth of the world's **cranes** make their home in Dubai.

WIND-TOWERS

Helping to keep houses still cooler was the wind-tower or *barjeel*. Developed uniquely in the Gulf, they were the earliest form of non-mechanical air conditioning. Generally built like a square tower, they stood at around 5m (16ft) high. Open on all four sides in order to catch the breezes, the tower contained a central shaft that funnelled the air downwards. Cooled by the downward motion, the air inside the tower then begins to pull the house's warmer air outside, setting up a natural process of convection. Wind-towers can be seen (and tried out) at the **Dubai Museum** and in **XVA Gallery** in Dubai and in the **Heritage Village** in Abu Dhabi.
SEE ALSO MUSEUMS AND GALLERIES, P.84, 88

MOSQUES

The very first mosque was modelled on the Prophet Mohammed's house. It was here that his followers would come to hear him preach or to pray.

Exterior

A mosque consists of an open courtyard *(sahn)*, arcaded portico *(riwaq)*, and a covered, often

Interior

Inside the mosque, a vaulted niche in the wall, the *mihrab*, indicates the direction of Mecca, towards which Muslims must face when praying, and the *minbar* serves as the pulpit from which imams (prayer leaders) preach the Friday sermon.

If you want to go inside a mosque, a worthwhile

Left: a classic wind-tower.
Right: Jumeira Mosque.

27

Not content with having invented the seven star category for hotels, Dubai's non-stop building upwards continues to add to the world's list of tallest hotels. The most recent addition is the 77 floor JW Marriott Marquis Dubai which opened January 2012 and stands at 355 metres (1,165 feet). Close behind and all in the top five tallest hotels worldwide are Dubai's Rose Rayhaan by Rotana, the Burj Al Arab and Jumeirah Emirates Tower Hotel.

experience, you can visit the **Jumeira Mosque** and the extraordinary **Grand Mosque** in Abu Dhabi.

MODERN ARCHITECTURE

The great majority of Dubai and Abu Dhabi's modern architecture is 'international' in style, made up of the 20th century's great building materials: concrete, glass and steel. Some of the buildings have been designed by the world's leading architects and are stunning in their visual impact – modern architecture aficionados will be in heaven. Stunning too, however, are the costs of cooling these enormous buildings, many of which have been designed without any consideration for the climate. Expensive to run, environmentally unfriendly and unlikely to endure, such buildings and building ethos are beginning to look somewhat out of step with the times.

However there is no arguing with the architectural ambition of Dubai. Whilst many fantastical projects have been cancelled or put on hold

Right: Yas Marina Circuit.

including the famous project, **The World** (between Deira and the Palm Jumeira, 300 man-made islands shaped to mirror a map of the world), the spectacular impression of the completed Burj Khalifa is enough to ensure Dubai will continue to impress with its futuristic designs.

FUTURE PROJECTS

DUBAI

Dubailand

Emirates Road; www.dubai land.ae; final phase: 2015–20
Comprising over 45 initiatives classing themselves as 'megaprojects', and a further 200 'subprojects', Dubailand is the most ambitious building project to date and will include at least 55 new luxury hotels.

Al Maktoum International Airport

Dubai World Central City, Jebel Ali; www.dwc.ae; expected to be completed and fully operational by 2017
Al Maktoum when finished will be the largest passenger – and cargo – hub on Earth. It is designed to handle more than 70 million passengers a year.

Nakheel Mall

Palm Jumeira; 2016
Nakheel Mall will contain nearly 200 shops, a nine-screen cinema and six medical clinics. There will be five retail levels and three basement parking levels with space for over 4,000 cars.

Sheikh Rashid Bin Saeed Crossing

Between Al Jadaaf district and Dubai Festival City; www.rta.ae; 2015
Measuring over 1,600m (5,200ft), the spectacular bridge will become the world's longest arch bridge.

ABU DHABI

Emirates Pearl

Al Khalidiya; 2014
Designed by Australian architect Dennis Lems, the 47-storey building is likely to become an iconic landmark. The building will contain a hotel, apartments and five restaurants.

Left: courtyard design.

The Gate District
Al Maqtaa district; ongoing development

Made up of a giant arch of eight towers, the District will also boast the Sky and Sun Towers. The Sky Tower is soon to be the city's tallest building and alongside it will be a five-star hotel, a mall and a waterside development which will include its own water adventure park.

ISLANDS
Desert Islands
www.desertislands.com
Various locations; 2014–18

This ambitious, joint tourism-commercial venture began with the establishment of the 'Arabian National Park' on Sir Bani Yas island (now open to guests of the Anatara Resort and Spa), and future plans are a heritage centre on Delma island and several protected areas designed to boost populations of turtles, birds and marine life. A

number of ecolodges and campsites will also be established.

Al Reem Island
300m/yds off northeast coast of Abu Dhabi; www.sorouh.com

This vast, multibillion-dollar SHAMS residential project will comprise several different districts and will eventually become the new home of over a quarter of a million people. In a landmark decision, property will be made available to all nationalities on an extendable 99-year leasehold.

Saadiyat Island
Northeast of Abu Dhabi Island; www.saadiyat.ae; 2018

Development is well underway on Saadiyat island and it will be home to around 30 new hotels, including a new, super-luxury 'seven star' hotel, three marinas, two golf courses and nearly 20km (12 miles) of beach. The much-vaunted Culture

District will be home to several museums and art centres, including its own Louvre museum and Guggenheim.

Yas Island
Hitting the headlines in 2009, the much-anticipated Formula One race track, Yas Marina Circuit, opened to host its first race. It is just one part of a giant leisure project that includes the first ever 'Ferrari World' theme park.

For those who can't resist checking out the view from level 124 of the world's tallest tower, head for the lower ground floor of the Dubai Mall. At the Top (tel: 04-888 8124; www.burjkhalifa.ae) is the name of the observation deck from which the city of Dubai can be seen with stunning 360° views. Open Sun–Wed 9am–midnight, Thur 8.30am–midnight, Fri–Sat 4.30am–midnight; admission charge under 3s free.

29

Bars and Cafés

Dubai and Abu Dhabi play a difficult double game: on the one hand pandering to the tastes of Western expats and tourists, on the other deferring to cultural and religious sensibilities at home. This is mostly played out in the cities' bars and pubs. Confined to the hotels, they're out of sight. For the visitor, this means missing out on nights at neighbourhood taverns, pub crawls or cocktails in beach huts by the sea. On the other hand, the hotels host some of the slickest, sleekest bars in the region, and there's no shortage of cafés. And for a genuine glimpse into local culture, there's always the *shisha* café. *See also Nightlife, p.90–95.*

DUBAI: DEIRA
Belgian Beer Café
Crowne Plaza Hotel, Dubai Festival City, near Business Bay Bridge; tel: 04-701 127; www.diningdfc.com; Sat–Wed noon–2am, Thur–Fri noon–3am; map p.135 D1
Styled like an old Belgian bistro, authenticity is the thing here: choose from a good selection of genuine Belgian beer washed down if you want with the traditional accompaniment, *moules* (mussels)

and *frites* (fries) served with mayonnaise. There are also branches at Grand Millenium hotel and at Madinat Jumeira.

Irish Village
The Aviation Club, near Al Garhoud Bridge; tel: 04-282 4750; www.irishvillage.ae; daily 11.30am–1am; map p.135 C3
Perennially popular among expats who love the outdoor terrace, the pub's well named: there's a great selection of Irish (and British) draught beers, Guinness-battered fish and chips and even a duck pond.

More
Behind Lifco Supermarket, Al Garhoud Road; tel: 04-283 0224; www.morecafe.biz; daily 8am–10pm; map p.135 C3
This family-friendly café attracts a fervent local following for its wide-ranging menu, imaginative food, freshness of its ingredients and generous portions,

---

Smoking
The smoking ban, introduced in January 2008, only allows smoking (including *shisha* smoking) in cafés, bars, pubs, nightclubs and restaurants with designated smoking areas (though not all have them), but outdoors on terraces is OK.

---

including doorstep- size sandwiches and super-size soups and salads, all served in its industrial chic interior. Branches of this popular chain also at Gold and Diamond Park, Dubai Mall, Mirdif City Centre, Mall of the Emirates and DIFC.

QD's
Dubai Creek Golf & Yacht Club, off Al Garhoud Road; tel: 04-295 6000; www.dubaigolf.com; daily 5pm–2am; map p.134 C3
This popular bar's biggest boon is its position right next to the Creek. Savour a sundowner or *shisha* whilst watching the *abras* or dhows chug by. For atmosphere Old Dubai-style, it's hard to beat.

Left: Belgian Beer Café.

Left: XVA Café.

the tongue quite as nicely as 'Singapore Sling', the Raffles 'Dubai Sling' is still worth tasting, particularly if it's whilst taking in the fabulous, panoramic views of the city (though the cocktail prices are almost as vertiginous).

Galler Chocolate Thé

Wafi Mall, Oud Metha Road; tel: 04-327 9120; Sun–Wed 10am–10pm, Thur–Sat 10am–midnight; map p.134 A1; Metro: Healthcare City
Hidden away in the neon depths of the Wafi Mall but well worth hunting for is this chocolate café, creation of legendary Belgian *chocolatier* Jean Galler. The decadent hot chocolate, crêpes, brownies or desserts are to die for Two shops are also open in Dubai Mall and Dubai Marina Mall.

XVA Café

Bastakia, off Al Seef Road; tel: 04-353 5383; www.xva hotel.com; May–Oct Sat–Thur 9am–7pm, Nov–Apr Sat–Thur 9am–7pm, Fri 10am–5pm; map p.130 B2; Metro: Al Fahidi
Tucked away in the heart of Bastakia, inside a traditional, 120-year-old courtyard house is the XVA. Making for an atmospheric, peaceful and laid-back vegetarian lunch stop on your way round the art galleries, its culinary mantra is 'simple, fresh, healthy and

The Terrace

Park Hyatt Dubai, Dubai Creek Golf and Yacht Club, Al Garhoud Road, tel: 04-317 2221; www.dubai.park.hyatt.com; daily noon–2am; map p.134 C3
Famous for its far-reaching views (across the yachts, marina, Creek and Dubai skyline), as well as its far-reaching cocktail and drinks list, The Terrace has become a firm favourite among local punters.

Vista

InterContinental Hotel, Festival City; tel: 04-701 1111; daily 8am–2am; map p.135 D1
Well named, the vodka and seafood bar boasts stunning views across the Creek from the chic confines of its cocktail-bar-cum-piano-lounge interior. There is also a terrace where you can smoke *shisha* in the evenings. Enticing eats are also available, though like the drinks, they don't come cheap.

BUR DUBAI
Arabian Tea House

Al Fahadi Street, Bastakia; tel:

04-353 5071; daily 8am–10pm; map p.130 B2; Metro Al Fahidi
Shaded by trees, spread with cushions and hung with Arabian lanterns and ornaments this is a traditional courtyard house of the Basta Art Gallery. It's a pleasant spot for a fruit juice, sandwich or just to rest sightseeing-weary legs.

Aroma Garden Caffe

Garden Home Building, Oud Metha Road; tel; 04-336 8999; daily 10am–2am; map p.134 A3; Metro: Oud Metha
Large, verdant and rambling, the Aroma has become a favourite haunt among those in the know for a spot of *shisha* smoking. If you fancy a puff, this is the place. If you're tired of all the shiny tourist traps, this is a quirky alternative.

Crossroads Cocktail Bar

Raffles Dubai, off Sheikh Rashid Road; tel: 04-324 8888; www.dubai.raffles.com; Sun–Thur 6pm–2am, Fri–Sat 6pm–3am; map p.134 A1; Metro: Healthcare City
Though it doesn't trip off

Dubai's pubs generally open from around midday and close around 1am during the week or 2am at the weekends. Bars tend to open later – around 4pm – in time to catch the post-work crowd – and close between 1am and 3am.

The distribution of alcohol in the UAE is a monopolised by just two companies, MMI and a+e. This, along with the expense of importing alcohol, which is heavily taxed, means that you might not always find your favourite tipple in Dubai and Abu Dhabi. Increasingly, however, themed bars, such as the Belgian Beer Café in Dubai and the Brauhaus in Abu Dhabi, are seeing the introduction of a greater variety of brands in bars.

nutritious'. It isn't the cheapest place, but the general ambience compensates. The café also has weekly film nights and has a dhow for rent; if you're alone, you can probably join another group.
SEE ALSO MUSEUMS AND GALLERIES, P.84

DUBAI: JUMEIRA
Bahri Bar
Mina A'Salam, Madinat Jumeirah hotel, Al Sufouh Road; tel: 04-366 6730; www.madinatjumeirah.com; Sat–Wed 4pm–2am, Thur–Fri 4pm–3am; map p.14
A strong contender for the best view of the Burj Al Arab award, the Bahri's also

worth a visit for the Disney-like, Aladdin-esque experience that is the Mina A'Salam and Madinat Jumeirah complex. Unreal during the day, it's positively surreal at night. It offers Arabian tapas and there's often a DJ or a band.

BarZar
Souk Madinat Jumeirah, Al Sufouh Road; tel: 04-366 6197; www.madinatjumeirah.com; Sun–Wed 6pm–2am, Thur–Fri 4pm–3am, Sat 4pm–2am; map p.14
Cavernous but cosy, urban-chic but fun, the two-storey BarZar is one of the most popular bars in the city, pulling in the hip young things by the *abra*-load. It also has a pleasant sofa-lined waterfront terrace and does enticing drinks deals.

Café Céramique
Town Centre Mall, Jumeira Road; tel: 04-344 7331; Sat–Thur 8am–midnight Fri 10am–midnight; map p.10
Half art gallery, half hip café, the award-winning Céramique is a great place for breakfast or lunch, serving good bagels, sandwiches and salads against a backdrop of ceramics

Many first-time visitors to the UAE worry about wetting their whistle. They needn't; alcohol is available in abundance and huge quantities are consumed daily by the cities' expat population – theoretically to alleviate the stress and strain of the 10- to 12-hour working days. You certainly pay for the privilege to drink; with import and other taxes of up to 50 percent on alcohol, an average bottle of wine can increase in price by 500 percent by the time it reaches you. Fortunately most bars and clubs offer special 'deals' and 'promotions', including short-spanned Happy Hours, and more famously, a ladies' night on Tuesdays when women drink free. With Dubai's male population currently touching 77 percent; bars and clubs are battling to woo the women. As a tourist, alcohol is only available in specially licensed premises, usually attached to the larger hotels or sports venues. Independent bars or pubs do not exist and nearly all restaurants outside hotels are dry. The restaurants in Madinat Jumeirah are some of the very few which do serve alcohol. Expats are allowed to purchase alcohol and drink in their homes, but first they must obtain a liquor license through their employer which they must show at the alcohol stores run by MMI and a+e.

which line the walls. If you should feel so inspired, you can head for the studio and pick up a paintbrush yourself. It's a hit with kids but you need to have a few days spare because anything you make needs to dry and then be fired in the kiln. There's another branch at Festival Centre (04-232 8616).

Right: The Agency.

Left Bank

Souk Madinat Jumeirah, Al Sufouh Road; tel: 04-368 6171; www.madinatjumeirah.com; daily noon–2am; map p.14
Though it feels more club than pub with its dim, neon-lit interior and minimalist design, it's enduringly popular for its range of drinks at competitive prices, buzzy atmosphere and attractive waterside terrace.

Lime Tree Café

Near Jumeira Mosque, Jumeira Road; tel: 04-349 8498; www.thelimetreecafe.com; daily 7.30am–6pm; map p.10
With a fanatical expat following, the ever-popular Lime Tree Café is one of the city's institutions. The pretty courtyard, ever-changing menu and wholesome homecooking at reasonable prices make for a fearsome formula: the carrot cake is legendary. Offshoots can also be found in the Ibn Battuta Mall west of Dubai Marina, in Al Quoz next to the Courtyard gallery, and Concord Tower in Dubai Media City.

Skyview Bar

Burj Al Arab hotel, Jumeira Road; tel: 04-301 7600; www.burj-al-arab.com; Sat–Thur noon–2am; map.14
With the 'seven star' hotel comes seven-star stipulations: a minimum spend of Dh250 for non-guests, a smart dress code (including no jeans) and compulsory reservations. But the blinding views from the top of the tower combined with

the chance to see inside the Burj ensure a steady stream of customers. Afternoon tea with a glass of bubbly is another option at Dh450 per person.
SEE ALSO HOTELS, P.71

DUBAI: SHEIKH ZAYED ROAD
The Agency

Ground Floor, Hotel Tower, Jumeirah Emirates Towers, Sheikh Zayed Road; tel: 04-319 8088; www.jumeirahemiratestowers.com; Sun–Thur 9am–1am, Fri–Sat 9am–midnight, map p. 12 Metro: Emirates Towers
Situated at the heart of the new financial centre, by day its coffee fuels the city

slickers and in the evening this upmarket wine bar brings in both local and international professionals. In the morning though lacking much atmosphere and fun, it gives a great glimpse of Dubai's bustling business scene and is a chance to see inside one of Dubai's most iconic buildings.

Cin Cin

Fairmont Dubai hotel; Sheikh Zayed Road; tel: 04-311 8316; www.fairmont.com; daily 6pm–2am, map p.132 B1; Metro: Trade Centre
With close to 350 varieties and vintages of wine, stacked in racks floor to ceiling, the plush and rar-

Left: Bahri Bar.
Right: Cin Cin.

Left: Trader Vic's.

Trader Vic's

Crowne Plaza Hotel Dubai, Sheikh Zayed Road; tel: 04-331 1111; www.tradervics.com; Sat–Thur noon–midnight, Fri noon 7pm–midnight; Metro: Emirates Tower

Something of a city institution, the curious combination of 'tropical' lounge, Polynesian music and famously lethal cocktails is as popular as ever, and has also spawned a few offshoots, such as the one at the Madinat Jumeirah.

efied wine bar attracts well-heeled, city oenophiles, who come also for the cigar bar next door.

Leftbank

Souk Al Bahar, Downtown Dubai; tel: 04- 368 4501; daily 6pm-2am

This bar brings in a trendy, youthful crowd. Popular and buzzy, it's a good bet for a relaxed drink.

Long's Bar

Towers Rotana Hotel, Sheikh Zayed Road; tel: 04-312 2202; www.rotana.com; daily noon–3am

Though boasting the longest bar in the Middle East, access to it isn't always assured: it's enduringly popular with expats. Traditional English pub in style, complete with pub grub, sport and darts, both food and drinks are reasonably-priced.

Organic Foods & Café

Dubai Mall, Downtown Burj Dubai, Sheikh Zayed Road; tel: 04-361 7974; www.organic foodsandcafe.com; daily 8am–8pm; map p.12; Metro: Burj Khalifa/ Dubai Mall

Dubai's first organic supermarket also runs a couple of small cafés that serve high-quality, flavoursome food along with delicious fruit juices and teas. A branch has newly opened in Dubai Mall.

Oscar's Vine Society

Next to Crowne Plaza hotel, Sheikh Zayed Road; tel: 04-331 1111; daily 6pm–midnight; Metro: Emirates Towers

A terrific haven from the heat, Oscar's is cool and cave-like, and boasts not just a well-stocked cellar, but delicious cheeses and charcuterie as well as imaginative main courses.

Vu's Bar

Jumeirah Emirates Towers hotel, Sheikh Zayed Road; tel: 04-330 8080; www.jumeirah emiratestowers.com; daily 6pm–3am; map p.12; Metro: Emirates Tower

The somewhat steep prices, stringent dress code ('smart') and required reservations are still worth it for the spectacular views overlooking the Sheikh Zayed strip. Situated on the 51st floor of the Jumeirah Emirates Towers, one of the tallest buildings in Dubai, the ride in the super-speedy elevator will make your ears pop.

Zyara Café

Union Tower, Sheikh Zayed Road; tel: 04-343 5454; daily 8am–1am

One of the city's most popular *shisha* cafés, the Zyara boasts a great location in the shadow of the sky-rises, and a brilliant bohemian décor, right down to the tangerine-coloured sofas. It attracts a mixed crowds of slickly dressed Lebanese businessmen (and women) texting and checking their laptops, locals playing backgammon and cards,

 Right: Vu's Bar.

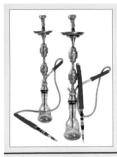

Shisha

The *shisha* (also known as a hookah, nargile and hubbly bubbly in other Arab regions) was originally introduced from Moghul India. Adopted by the ruling classes, they soon became an essential accessory of the rich and fashionable right across the Middle East. In the Arab world, rather like the Western pub, *shisha* cafés serve as social gathering places of the city's citizens. Usually male-dominated, they're spots where business is discussed and news and gossip exchanged over a coffee, tea or game of backgammon. Most cafés in Dubai and Abu Dhabi offer *shishas*, and some bars, lounges and clubs have a designated *shisha* area, where you can chill out on comfy sofas, often with a sea view and breeze to boot. A *shisha* café can give a visitor a real glimpse of local culture. If you want to smoke a *shisha* (essentially tobacco infused with an aromatic flavour of your choice ranging from rose to peppermint and strawberry), a *shisha* session (which can last an hour or more) will typically cost Dh15–30 although in the upmarket hotels it's closer to Dh50. Though forming part of Middle Eastern culture for centuries, the *shisha* café's future is not firmly assured. In February 2008, Abu Dubai stopped issuing new *shisha* café licences in a bid to 'protect public health'.

and young Emirati women having a gossip, amid the mellow, aromatic smoke of the *shisha*. There's another branch at Media City.

DUBAI MARINA
Bar 44
Grosvenor House hotel, West Marina Beach, Al Sufouh Road; tel: 04-399 8888; www.grosvenorhouse-dubai.com; Fri–Wed 6pm–2am, Thur 6pm–3am; map p.14

A serious contender for best view of New Dubai, Bar 44 is named after its dizzying position (and prices) on the 44th floor of the Grosvenor. Chic and smart, it attracts cigar-smoking, champagne-quaffing customers who like the mellow atmosphere and piano tinkling and/or jazz singing.

Barasti Bar
Le Meridien Mina Seyahi, Al Sufouh Road; tel: 04-318 1313; www.barastibeach.com; daily 11.30am–1.15am; map p.14

One of the most popular beachside bars in Dubai, expats love the setting, views and informality. Cush-

ions, beanbags and loungers litter the beach area, ensuring a mood that's laid-back, friendly and fun. It's a good place to settle down to a *shisha* too.

Buddha Bar
Grosvenor House, West Marina Beach, Al Sufouh Road; tel: 04-399 8888; www.grosvenorhouse-dubai.com; Sat–Wed 8pm–2am, Thur–Fri 8pm–3am; map p.14

A favourite hang-out for Dubai's 'beautiful people', the bar-cum-restaurant has a reputation for great music, cocktails and Asian-fusion food, served up in chic and seductive surroundings.

Café Bateel
Marina Walk tel: 04-368 4696; daily 8am–11.30pm

Even cafés in Dubai aren't immune from the five-star frenzy. The popular Café Bateel serves date-inspired dishes of all types (from salads and pasta dishes to ice creams) in a lavish café. The Arabic coffee and delicious date-made cakes are well worth a stop.

Below: Rooftop Lounge & Terrace.

Left: Heroes.
Below: Captain's Arms.

(served from 4–6pm daily) is not a bad way. There's a Dhs100 per person minimum spend. You can admire the dazzling decor over a sandwich and scone whilst watching the well-heeled world trip by.

Cristal Cigar & Champagne Bar
Millennium Hotel, Khalifa Street; tel: 02-614 6020; daily 5pm–2am; map p.137 D3
As the name says, this is the place for a cigar, some champagne or fine wine. Somewhat 'gentleman's club' in feel, the rarified atmosphere is fun if you feel like a bit of indulgence. Good 'finger food' is available, the service is attentive and a piano tinkles in the background.

Emporio Armani Café
Mall of the Emirates, Sheikh Zayed Road, Via Rodeo; tel: 04-341 0591; daily 11am–11.30pm; map p.14; Metro: Mall of the Emirates
As chic as the clothes of its namesake, the café also has a reputation for good Italian cooking at reasonable prices and is a great place for a plate of pasta or a reviving Italian espresso in between the shopping.

Oeno
The Westin Dubai Mina Seyahi, Al Sufouh Road; tel: 04-399 4141; www.westinminaseyahi. com; Mon 7pm–1.30am, Tue 6pm–1.30am, Wed 8pm–1.30am, Thur–Fri 6pm–2.30am, Sat 6pm–1.30am; map p.14
Satisfying even serious wine (and cheese) buffs, Oeno boasts probably the best cellar in the city. You can either tuck into a glass or two of your favourite tipple, or get stuck into some serious wine and cheese tasting.

Rooftop Lounge & Terrace
One&Only Royal Mirage, Al Sufouh Road; tel: 04-399 9999; www.royalmirage.oneandonly resorts.com; daily 5pm–1am;

map p.14
With fabulous views over the Palm Jumeira and the Gulf, with an intimate atmosphere of candles, cushions and cosy booths, and a good selection of both cocktails and beers, this is arguably Dubai's best bar. It's certainly a great place to while away a warm evening.

ABU DHABI: CORNICHE
The Café
Emirates Palace Hotel, Corniche West; tel: 02-690 7999; www. emiratespalace.com; daily 6.30am–1am; map p.136 A3
If you want to gain a small insight into the 'Pink Palace', afternoon tea

Havana Café
Near Marina Mall, Breakwater; tel: 02-681 0044; daily 9am–2am; map p.136 B3
With its stunning views across the waterfront to the high-rises on the Corniche, the little Havana challenges (and probably beats) the more famous five-stars for the best view in Abu Dhabi award. With its great atmosphere, a rooftop terrace and *shisha* in cooler months and flavoursome Arabic fare, it's a must.

Heroes
Crowne Plaza Hotel, Sheikh Hamdan bin Mohamed St; tel: 02-616 6101; daily noon–2.30am; map p.137 D2
Wildly popular with the expat crowd who congregate for the sports coverage, it's also a friendly, informal and fun place

serving pub grub and beer at reasonable prices.

Jazz Bar
Corniche Hilton Abu Dhabi, Corniche Road West; tel: 02-681 1900; daily 7.30pm–1.30am; map p.136 B3
Something of an Abu Dhabi institution, this bar-cum-restaurant is known for the quality of its live jazz performances as well as its wine, cocktail and drinks list, and fine food.

CENTRAL AND SOUTH ABU DHABI
Brauhaus
Beach Rotana Hotel, near Abu Dhabi Mall, Tourist Club Area; tel: 02-697 9000; www.rotana.com; Sun–Wed 4pm–1am dinner 4pm–11.30pm, Thur–Sat noon-1am food noon–11.30pm; map p.139 E2
Styled like an authentic German bar, Brauhaus also serves genuine German beer, which brings in a loyal group of expats. German-style food is also available if you're suddenly hankering after sausages.

Captain's Arms
Le Meridien Abu Dhabi, Sheikh Zayed the Second Street; tel: 02-644 6666; www.lemeridien abudhabi.com; daily noon–1am; map p.137 E3
Another old favourite among the city's expats, the Captain draws in a steady crowd for its outdoor terrace, Happy Hour (occurring 5–10pm daily), its decent pub grub generously served, and its informal, cosy atmosphere styled on a typical British pub.
Le Boulanger
BHS Building, Hamdan Bin Mohamed St; tel: 02-626 2700; daily 8am–8pm; map p.137 D3
True to its name, the centrally located French café-cum bakery produces great croissants, baguettes, cakes, quiches and tarts, but you can also sit down to breakfast or lunch here whilst perusing the papers. Appetising mains and desserts are also served. There's another branch (tel: 02-681 8194) at Breakwater Road just around the bend of the road going towards Marina Mall. It serves Arabic fare, sandwiches and pasta and you can smoke *shisha* there too.

P.J. O'Reilly's
Le Royal Méridien, Khalifa Street; tel: 02-674 2020; www.leroyalmeridienabud-habi.com; daily noon–2.30am; map p.137 D3
Much loved locally for its boisterous and friendly vibe, and decent pub grub served in ample portions and at respectable prices, PJ's is also famous for its earlier-than-most Happy Hour (from midday to 8pm daily).

Trader Vic's
Beach Rotana Hotel, near Abu Dhabi Mall, 9th Street; tel: 02-

697 9011; daily 12.30pm–3pm, bar 6pm–1.30am, dinner 7pm–midnight; map p.137 E2
Another Abu Dhabi institution, this French Polynesian-themed bar-cum-restaurant has built a solid reputation based on flavoursome food, assiduous service, lethal cocktails and good, tropical fun.

Zyara Café
Next to Hilton Corniche Residence; tel: 02-627 5006; daily 8am–midnight
Affectionately dubbed the 'Little Red Café' after its bright and colourful interior, the Zyara is popular locally for its Bohemian feel and views over the Corniche. It's a good spot for breakfast or lunch, though it's not the cheapest place and the food can be a little variable.

Right: P.J. O'Reilly's.

Children

D ubai and Abu Dhabi are two of the most child-friendly cities in the world. With year-round sunshine, safe, sandy beaches, locals who love children, and some great theme parks, there's plenty to keep kids amused. The town's hotels and malls fall over themselves to offer facilities for families – from babysitting services to topnotch sport facilities. Many restaurants also offer play areas, as well as kids' menus. Above all, the cities are very safe places; just beware the busy roads and the sun's scorching rays. To save money, look out for the locally produced discount book *The Entertainer*. as many attractions are half price using its coupons.

BABYSITTING

Many of the four and five-star hotels offer babysitting services; they cost around Dh80–100 for three to four hours. Most of the cities' malls also offer child supervision. However be aware that this usually means the children can play in a secure soft play area with other children of mixed ages so this would not be recommended for very young children who need constant attention.

FACILITIES

Childcare facilities match or even better those in the West, though not all restaurants have high-chairs. Nappy-changing facilities can be found in the women's toilets in malls and some restaurants.

AMUSEMENT CENTRES AND ARCADES

DUBAI

Children's City
Creekside Park, Riyadh Road; tel: 04-334 0808; www. childrencity.ae; Sat–Thur 9am–

8pm, Fri 3–9pm; admission charge although under 2s free; map p.134 B2
A municipality-run science museum-cum-amusement park, this interactive 'info-tainment' centre – the fifth-largest in the world – is well-designed and imaginatively done; it's also fun. Comprising diverse zones ranging from a planetarium to the 'Nature Center' and 'International Culture' gallery, it's designed to appeal to all ages, from toddlers to teenagers. A few of the exhibits are on their last legs but that

shouldn't deter you, it's a good deal. Creekside or Creek Park is also home to the **Dubai Dolphinarium**, (www.dubaidolphinarium.ae) another municipality attraction.

Encounter Zone

Level 3, Wafi City Mall, Oud Metha Road; tel: 04-324 7747; Thur–Sat 10am–midnight, Sun–Wed 10am–10pm; admission charge; map p.134 A1; Metro: Healthcare City
Comprising two parts – Lunar Park, basically a soft play area with themed rides and slides for kids between one and eight, and Galactica, which includes a skate park, video games, a 3D cinema and the mentally challenging Crystal Maze (designed for teenagers to adults), Encounter Zone is a great place to keep kids amused while you shop up a storm; there's a babysitting service.

Magic Planet

Deira City Centre Mall; tel: 04-295 4333; www.playmania. com/magicplanet; daily 10am–

include a space maze, 3D theatre and 3D games. Like many of Dubai's other centres, it's designed to educate and entertain, to exercise and amuse.

ABU DHABI

Fun City
Marina Mall, Breakwater; tel: 02-681 5527; daily 10am–10pm; free admission, charge for rides ; map p.136 B3
A funfair-cum-arcade, Fun City appeals to older kids as well as little ones, mainly due to its high-tech computer and video games. It's a popular place for shopping expat Mums offloading kids for a couple of hours.

MUSEUMS AND HERITAGE CENTRES

DUBAI

Dubai Museum
Al Fahidi Fort, off Al Fahidi Square, Bastakia; tel: 04-353 1862; www.dubaitourism.ae; Sat–Thur 8.30am–8.30pm, Fri 2.30–8.30pm; admission charge; map p.130 B2; Metro Al Fahidi
A hit with most young children are the dioramas in the museum's basement (particularly the recreated souk) complete with

---

Children of all ages seem to love the novelty of cramming on an *abra* with all the city's commuters and chugging across the Creek (Dh1). Hang on to little children, as there's very little between them and the water and no safety provisions. You may fancy hiring an *abra* as a family.

---

midnight; free admission, charge for rides; map p.134 C4; Metro Deira: City Centre
An unabashed orgy of arcade games and classic fairground rides including dodgems, a merry-go-round and a big wheel, the ever-popular Magic Planet appeals particularly to pre-teen kids (though the ten-pin bowling alley may amuse teens). There's also a soft play area for toddlers, and a good range of eateries in the food court, from where you can watch your kiddies without the same level of noise.

Peekaboo
2nd Floor, Magic Planet, Mall of the Emirates; tel: 04-347 0622;

---

www.peekaboo.ae; admission charge; daily 10am–9pm; map p.14
This is a separate, enclosed play area which offers a gentler environment where babies and children up to the age of seven can play creatively. There are toys such as dolls and cars as well as activities on offer like art, cookery and singing. Johnny Rockets with its tasty burgers and excellent milkshakes is conveniently next door if kids need refuelling. There's another branch of Peekaboo in the Village Mall on Jumeira Road tel: 04-344 7122; daily 9am–8pm.

Stargate
Za'abeel Park, Sheikh Zayed Road; tel: 04-398 6888; admission charge; Sun–Thur 10am–10pm, Fri–Sat 10am–midnight; p.133 D2; Metro: Al Jaffiliya
Amusement park meets *Star Trek*, Stargate is modelled on a crash-landed spaceship, with quite high-tech attractions that

---

Dubai's many municipal parks are well-kept and very pleasant places to explore in the cooler months. There are playgrounds for younger children. Za'abeel, Safa and Mushrif (which is near Mirdif City Centre Mall) are all recommended. There's a small charge to enter. Locals take enormous picnics and sit under the trees.

If you visit the cities during the stifling summer months, do as the locals do and head for the **malls**. They're not only air-conditioned to the point of iciness, but they also bend over backwards to accommodate children. All malls have at least one play area, which ranges from funfair-style rides to high-tech arcades and sandpits. Many malls additionally put on children's entertainment, such as puppet shows, face-painters and clowns, as well as changing organised events such as treasure hunts, storytelling tours and children's classes. In their shrewd drive to offer all things to all customers (and keep them shopping), many of Dubai and Abu Dhabi's malls also offer a 'shop and drop' service to parents of young children keen for a couple of hours of hassle-free shopping. Centres are supervised, often have secure gates and follow careful ID procedures. If you visit a mall, enquire about its facilities and activities.

spooky lighting, spicy smells and sound effects. The display on the gruelling job of pearl fishing and the array of authentic pearling boats in the courtyard, as well as the old *khanjars* (knives) and rifles might amuse the boys, young and old.
SEE ALSO MUSEUMS AND GALLERIES, P.84

Heritage & Diving Village
Off Al Khaleej Road, Al Shindagha; tel: 04-393 7151; www.dubaitourism.ae; Sun–Thur 8.30am–10.30pm, Fri–Sat 8am–10.30pm; free; map p.130 A3
During the Dubai shopping festivals, the twin villages come alive with live displays of singing, dancing

and storytelling, as well as other traditional demonstrations including rifle throwing. Kids can also ride camels and donkeys and sample traditional food and beverages. Outside the festivals, the place can be quiet; check in advance of a visit.
SEE ALSO MUSEUMS AND GALLERIES, P.84

THEME PARKS AND WATERPARKS

DUBAI

Aquaventure & the Lost Chambers
Atlantis hotel, Palm Jumeirah; tel: 04-426 0000; www.atlantis thepalm.com; Aquaventure daily 10am–sunset, Lost Chambers daily 10am–10pm; admission charge under 2s free; map p.14
Highlights of this new hotel's excellent water park include the 'Ziggurat', a 27.5m (90ft)-high near-vertical slide that sends visitors through 'shark-infested waters' (albeit in an acrylic tube submerged in a pool), and a 2.3km- (1½ -mile) long 'river ride' which transports rubber ring-lounging bathers through a 'tropical landscape' with rapids, wave surges and cascades along the way. Atlantis's

Lost Chambers is an aquarium-cum-theme park set in a warren of underwa-

Dubai and Abu Dhabi boast many world-beating statistics, including a few they may be less proud of. These include some of the highest incidences of pedestrian deaths anywhere. In the first half of 2012, over 80 pedestrians were killed in both cities. By the end of the year, there had been 151 deaths and 934 injured in 954 pedestrain-vehicle incidents. The cities' main problems are heavy traffic, town planning that is notoriously pedestrian-unfriendly, local women who are afraid to use subways, and low driving standards, including road-rule flouting and young, inexperienced Emirati (and expats) boys driving some of the world's most powerful cars. Fortunately plans are afoot to rectify these problems, including Abu Dhabi's ambitious new 'Streetscape' 2030 plan which intends to create walkable neighbourhoods. In the meantime, pay careful attention when crossing roads, and keep a very sharp eye on children. Note also that jaywalking now incurs a stiff fine of Dh200; in 2011, 37 484 jaywalkers were fined and around 750 fines are issued by Abu Dhabi police every month.

Left: Lost Chambers.

ter halls and tunnels which boasts over 250 species of marine creature, including sharks, moray eels and piranhas. Atlantis is also the home of Dolphin Bay *(see p.15)* and sosphisticated separate kids and teens clubs.

Al Nasr Leisureland

Behind American Hospital, Oud Metha; tel: 04-337 1234; www.alnasrll.com; daily 9am–10.30pm as a general rule but closing times vary from dusk to midnight depending on sport so do check in advance; admission charge; map p.133 E2

Designed as a sports-cum-entertainment complex, the Al-Nasr Leisureland is a good choice if you've got teens keen to let off steam and younger children demanding entertainment. The sport facilities accommodate ice skating, tennis, squash, bowling and swimming (including a pool with a wave machine, water slides and cannons), and the Luna Park offers the usual funfair faves including dodgems, go-karting and a roller coaster.

Ski Dubai Snow Park

Mall of the Emirates, Sheikh Zayed Road; tel: 800–FUN, Snow Penguins 04-409 4090; www.skidxb.com; admission charge; Ski Dubai Sun–Wed 10am–11pm, Thur 10am–midnight, Fri 9am–midnight, Sat 9am–11pm; Penguin Encounters Sun–Thur 1–9pm, Fri–Sat noon–9pm, map p.14; Metro: Mall of the Emirates

Perverse it may be, but kids love Ski Dubai. With its

snow and skiing, as well as tobogganing, play area, snowmen, snowballs and Christmas trees, it seems to gratify children of all ages. It's also makes the best escape imaginable from soaring summer temperatures – try building a snowman in August. Though called a 'park', it's actually an indoor centre (albeit the third-largest indoor snow dome in the world, containing no less than 6,000 tonnes of snow), so it offers just five runs (ranging from beginners' to the world's first indoor 'Black'). It can get crowded; try to avoid the weekends (Friday and Saturday). All gear is included in the price of your pass (from skis, boots and snowboards to jackets, trousers, children's helmets and socks). Dress warm as

well as little ones especially chill quickly in this environment. Lockers can be rented. To use the slopes, you need to be able to demonstrate basic proficiency (the ability to stop, turn, controlling speed and use the tow and chairlift). For beginners, lessons are offered by certified instructors (from Dh160 per hour for a group lesson for 3-6 year olds). You can watch your little ones whizz down (or wipe out on) the slopes from the Alpine-inspired café-cum-bar, **Après** (tel: 04-341 2575; daily noon–1am), which overlooks the far end of the dome. It's a great place for a hot chocolate or a *glüwein*, and also does food for ravenous kids post-winter sport cavorting. Adults will also enjoy the cocktails.

Right: Wild Wadi Waterpark, *see p.42.*

41

which visitors can body or knee surf, which has become a bit of a hit with local teenagers who compete for how long they can 'ride the waves', and **Breakers Bay** the largest wave pool in the Middle East. Look out also for **Wadi Wash**. Every hour on the hour, no less than 60,000 litres (13,000 gallons) of water are tipped from 'Fossil Rock' to create a flash-flood effect, complete with choreographed thunder sound-effects. Designed especially for small children is **Juha's Dhow**, a kind of climbing frame-cum-waterpark with milder water rides and squeal-inducing dumping buckets and squirting cannons. Wild Wadi's facilities include lots of lifeguards, changing rooms, showers and cafés and fast-food outlets. Try to come during the week (Sun–Thur) to avoid the queues.

SEGA Republic Indoor Theme Park

Level 2, Dubai Mall; tel: 04-448 8484; www.segarepublic.com; Sun–Wed 10am–11pm, Thur–Sat 10am–1am; admission charge, free for children under 90 cm; map p. 12; Metro: Burj Khalifa/Dubai Mall

Complete with a roller-coaster, motion simulators, big heart-thumping rides and more amusement games than you could ever play, SEGA is good for older children. There's also a SEGA Republic Game-Zone at Marina Mall.

Wild Wadi Waterpark

Off Jumeira Road, near the Jumeirah Beach Hotel; tel: 04-348 4444; www.wildwadi.com; Nov–Feb 10am–6pm, Mar–May 10am–7pm, June–Aug 10am–8pm, Sept–Oct 10am–7pm; admission charge, under 2s free; map p.10

Unquestionably this is the most popular children's attraction in Dubai. Encompassing 4.8 hectares (12 acres), Wild Wadi is on the small side compared to similar American water-parks, but the rides and attractions (now 30) are certainly packed in, and there's something to please all ages. The park takes its

theme from the Arabian tale of Juha the adventurer (and his friend Sinbad), and rides range from the locally famed **Jumeirah Sceirah** – at 33m (108ft), it is the highest and fastest near-freefall ride outside the US – to the more sedate **Juha's Journey**, in which visitors are floated on rubber rings down a 360m (1180ft) 'river'. Considered other highlights are **Wipeout FlowRider** – one of only four of its kind in the world – a wave pool in

If there's one mall which could occupy children for days on end, it's Mirdif City Centre (www. mirdifcitycentre.com). It's ten minutes by taxi from Festival Centre or the airport. For younger kids, it has a play area called Little Explorers (www.the-playmania.com), lots of water-based amusement at Aqua Play, and Cité des Enfants which is another edutainment venue focusing on learning and discovery in a fun way. For amusement and rides there's Magic Planet. For the active or adventurous there's Soccer Circus, bowling, a climbing wall and i-Fly where you can try indoor skydiving. When everyone's exhausted you can catch a film.

ABU DHABI

Ferrari World

Ferrari World, Yas Island; tel: 02-249 8000; www.ferrari worldabudhabi.com; Tue–Sun 11am–8pm: admission charge

This is the world's largest indoor theme park, complete with shopping facilities and Italian restaurants. With its 20 attractions and rides including the world's fastest rollercoaster and a flight simulator, Ferrari World should appeal to daredevil older children. There are activities for younger children; junior racers can learn to drive in Ferrari cars, sized especially for kids, and at the

Junior Training Camp little ones can play in the waterless carwash and pilot remote controlled cars.

Wanasa Land

Al Wahdah Mall, 11th Street; tel: 2-443 7654; www.wanasa land.com; Wed–Sat 10am–10pm, Thur–Fri 10am–1am; free, charges for rides; map p. 137 D1

Combining a soft play area and funfair rides varying in thrill-intensity with more high-tech computer games as well, this centre is aimed at children of all ages. There's also a shooting range with electronic guns.

WILDLIFE

DUBAI

Dubai Aquarium & Underwater Zoo

Dubai Mall, Near the Burj Dubai; tel: 04-437 3200; www.thedubaimall.com; Sun–Wed 10am–midnight, Thur–Sun 10am–midnight; mall free, Aquarium & Zoo admission charge; map p.12; Metro: Burj Khalifa/Dubai Mall

The new Aquarium is spectacular for its size as well as its enormous view ing panel, which at nearly 34m (111ft) wide and over 8m (26ft) high, is the largest in the world. Inside, over 33,000 marine animals swim, including sharks and rays, and running through it is a 270-degree, walk-through tunnel complete with 'lunar-cyclic' lighting that varies with the day.

The Underwater Zoo on the top floor of the Mall is an aquarium-cum-zoo split into different ecological zones (from Rainforest to Rocky Shore), and the live exhibits range from piranhas to otters, harbour

seals and Humboldt penguins (though living in rather cramped confines). The mall also contains an ice rink.

KidZania

Level 2, Dubai Mall, opposite Reel Cinemas; tel: 04-448 5222; www.kidzania.ae; Sun–Wed 9am–midnight, Thur 9am–1am, Fri–Sat 10am–1am; admission charge, under 2s free; map p.12; Metro: Burj Khalifa/ Dubai Mall

A scaled-down city in which kids can play at being grown-ups, with a choice of 75 professions ranging from banker to bus driver and construction worker. There's even a special kid economy and currency, the KidZo. From an educational point of view, this is the perfect place for children to enjoy role playing and they leave with their own driving licenses and wads of KidZo cash which they earn for their hard work. Some have argued that there is a lot of sponsorship inside KidZania and the cynics would say it's all about getting children and their parents to recognise certain brands. However, it's definitely a fun experience for imaginative children and there's a toddler-friendly zone and baby care centre. It does become expensive as parents have to pay to accompany their children.

Ras Al Khor Wildlife Sanctuary

Off Oud Metha Road, Ras Al Khor; tel: 04-606 6822; www.wildlife.ae; Sat–Thur

9am–4pm, 9am–2pm during Ramadam

If your kid's eyes are square with video games, or you're just after a bit of down time after city excitements, the Ras Al Khor Sanctuary makes a lovely break. Hides allow you to get quite close to the birds, and most kids love watching the pink flamingos search for food amid the mangroves and mud flats. Most birds are seen first thing in the morning or last thing in the afternoon. At 9.20am and 4.20pm the birds are fed. During the summer months, the flamingos can be scarce. Park wardens can lend binoculars (an added novelty) as well as answer the endless questions. Species include several types of heron, sandpiper and plover, as well as greenshanks.

SEE ALSO ENVIRONMENT, P.50

For those families who have access to a car during their stay in Dubai it's worth taking a road trip to the Arabian Wildlife Centre in Sharjah. Over 100 animal species are on display here and much of it is indoors.

Right: the Atlantis runs regular kids' clubs, as do other major hotels.

Desert Excursions

Difficult as it may be to imagine within the chilly confines of the malls or the rolling greens of the golf courses, the desert is just a stone's throw away. A visit here gives a graphic idea not just of pre-oil Arabia, but also the reality of traditional Bedouin life, and the lightning-quick development of Dubai and Abu Dhabi. If you've never experienced the vast expanses, emptiness, silence and tranquillity of the desert, it will make an indelible impression. The legendary Rub Al Khali, the Empty Quarter, is the largest sea of sand on the planet. Local tour companies offer various desert activities.

SAFARIS

On a safari, a good guide can give precious insights into traditional Bedouin life, desert wildlife, ecology and traditional Emirati culture. Unfortunately, not all companies provide knowledgeable guides. Choose a reputable agency and ensure your guide is properly qualified.

Tour companies offer half-day trips, full-day trips, or longer. Half-day trips (usually from around 4pm to 10pm) generally include some dune driving, a visit to a camel farm and a buffet-style, 'Bedouin' desert-dinner with all the tourist trimmings: camel rides, traditional music, *shisha* smoking and a belly dancer. Full-day tours include the above, plus a trip to the town of Hatta from Dubai plus the Hajar Mountains. Day trips from Abu Dhabi also include the Hajar Mountains.

For a more meaningful – and memorable – desert safari, consider overnighting in the desert (full camping equipment and all meals are provided). If there's a group of you, consider suggesting your own itinerary.

Due to stiff competition between agencies, prices are very reasonable, but beware bargains, as standards of tour companies vary considerably. Most companies require a minimum of two people for a trip and will often amalgamate singles or a couple into another group.

DUBAI

Arabian Adventures
Emirates Holidays Building, Sheikh Zayed Road; tel: 04-303 4888; www.arabian-adventures.com
One of the largest and most reputable tour companies in the UAE, guides are generally decent, and a good variety of safaris and activities are offered.

Lama Tours
Al Sayegh Building, Oud Metha

Left: organised excursions let you safely explore the desert.

Left: riding over the dunes near Dubai.

shovel, a first-aid kit, a supply of food and at least 5 litres (9 pints) of water per person. A useful guide that's published (and available) locally is *UAE Off-Road Explorer*.

CAR HIRE

4WDs are easily hired from Dubai and Abu Dhabi's tour companies, many of which have 24-hour outlets at the airport, including those below. Drivers must be 25 years or over to hire a 4WD (21 years for smaller cars).

Road, Bur Dubai; tel: 04-334 4330; www.lamadesert tours.com

Another dependable company, Lama Tours offers all the standard desert safaris including over-nighters inclusive of a BBQ buffet.

ABU DHABI

Net Tours
Opposite Sheraton Abu Dhabi, Khalifa Street; tel: 02-679 4658; www.nettoursuae.ae; map p.137 D3
One of the oldest tour companies in the Emirates, Net has built a solid reputation and offers a comprehensive range of safaris and tours, as well as desert activities.

DESERT DRIVING

Also known as 'dune bashing', the activity is almost a national sport in Dubai and Abu Dhabi. The most popular spot around Dubai is on the dunes off the Dubai–Hatta road and particularly at a dune christened **'Big Red'**, lying around 30 minutes outside the city.

Below: fascinating patterns that shift with the wind.

The largest dune in the UAE, Moreeb Hill, is found in Liwa lying on the edge of the great Empty Quarter in the far south of the Emirates. It's most easily accessed from Abu Dhabi and it takes approximately two hours to drive.

If you're new to desert driving, it's advisable to follow a few basic safety rules: drive with preferably two other vehicles and make sure the tank is full, bring maps, a tow rope,

Many visitors to the Emirates are shocked by the state of the scenery. Though the cities may be kept sparkling by the legions of immigrant labourers, not so their countryside. Every year, several hundred camels die in both emirates from the ingestion of plastic bags. Until relatively recently, UAE waste was biodegradable. Consisting of organic material such as pottery, cotton or paper, the Bedu didn't have to worry about waste. With the discovery of oil and the introduction of plastics along with a consumer culture, bygone Bedouin ways began to come back to haunt them. Meanwhile, the desert's fragile eco-structure is suffering at the wheels of the weekend 4WDs that pour out of Emirati cities for desert driving and dune bashing. Normally home to hundreds of species, nothing survives in the continually churned topsoil. Conservation groups are campaigning to limit off-driving to certain areas. In the meantime, visitors can reduce their impact by sticking to established tracks and dunes.

'Bedu' means 'nomadic', after the old way of living. After pitching the traditional camel or goat-hair tent, the *beit ash-sha'ar* (literally 'house of hair'), the **Bedu** (plural of Bedouin) would graze their goats, sheep or camels for up to several months. When the sparse grazing ran out, the Bedu would move on, allowing the land to regenerate naturally. The tents were divided into two areas: a *haram* (forbidden) area reserved for women, and a men's section which also served as the *majlis* – the place to receive and entertain guests. It was here that all news and gossip was exchanged, a crucial part of successful desert survival. For water, the Bedu faced long walks to wells or springs. For food, they lived off camel's milk, dates, goat meat and sometimes a hare or other game caught with falcons. Part of the ancient and sacrosanct Bedouin creed was that no stranger in need of rest or food should be turned away. For three days the guest was assured protection with no obligation even to impart his name. He was also guaranteed safe passage through tribal territory. Such a strict code of protocol ensured the survival of all in a very hostile environment with scant resources. The legendary hospitality of the Arabs today is directly derived from their Bedu days.

DUBAI

Avis

Al Maktoum Road, Deira; tel: 04-295 7121; www.avis.com; Sat–Thur 8am–7pm, Fri 4–9pm
Avis offers a good choice of car and free pick-up and delivery to your hotel or airport (within Dubai).

ABU DHABI

Avis

Royal Jet Terminal, Abu Dhabi International airport; tel: 02-575 7180; www.avis.com; 24 hours
Avis Abu Dhabi also boasts various city branches plus a pick-up and drop-off service and a good variety of cars and 4WDs.

DESERT DRIVING COURSES

If you've never driven off-road before, a couple of hours of instruction is highly recommended and makes a great introduction to the activity. Instructors are professional and well qualified. Individual and group tuition is usually available, but drivers must be 25 years old or above.

DUBAI

Explorer Tours

tel: 04-286 1991; www.explorertours.ae
The company offers a variety of tours and if you own a 4WD, it's possible to do a desert driving course with them.

ABU DHABI

Nomad 4x4

tel: 04-450 2429; www.nomad4x4.com
This company is based in Dubai but can arrange desert driving courses in Abu Dhabi.

CAMEL AND HORSE RIDING

Though a bit hackneyed and over-hyped, camel rides are fun, particularly for kids. They also provide the 'me-on-a-camel' photo that's obligatory for some. All the main tour operators *(see 'Desert Safaris' above)* can organise both camel and horse riding, including excursions into the desert lasting an hour or more. Note that some people start to feel a bit saddle sore after an hour (or less) on their furry mounts.

QUAD BIKING

Quad bikes are available for hire at the popular dune-bashing spots,

.eft and below: camels, balloons and 4WDs can take you there, but don't miss the desert sunset.

including Dubai's Big Red. Most rental companies offer customers a choice of 50cc, 80cc and 100cc bikes and are open from 8am to sunset daily.

SAND SKIING AND BOARDING

Growing ever more in popularity both locally and abroad, various companies offer dedicated sand boarding (and some, sand skiing) trips, or as part of another tour, and provide full equipment and instruction. Similar in technique to snow skiing and boarding, you'll have a softer fall, and you won't have to worry about the cold, but you will about the sun which, reflected off the dunes, can be dazzling. This activity is best done in the morning when the temperatures are lower. Sunglasses and sun block are essential.

DUBAI

Desert Rangers
Dubai Garden Centre, off Sheikh Zayed Road, Al Quoz; tel: 04-357 2200; www.desertrangers.com; Sat–Thur 8am–7pm, Fri 4–9pm
This reputable company offers sand-boarding safaris as well as dune buggy trips among others.

ABU DHABI

Arabian Adventures
Mezzanine Floor, Emirates Travel Shop, Corniche Road; tel: 02-691 1711; www.arabian-adventures.com; daily 9am–6.30pm; map p.136 B3
Part of the country-wide group, the company boasts a good reputation and a decent range of desert safaris and activities including sand-boarding and sand-skiing safaris and camel riding.

Dhows

For millennia, the ancient trading vessel, the dhow, has provided a crucial link between the Gulf, Africa and Asia. Unmistakable on the water for its squat shape and triangular sail, this boat has played no small part in the history of Dubai and Abu Dhabi. Built on its bulbous hulls were the fortunes not just of its merchant seamen, but even of whole ports and cities. Today, dhows still brave the waters of the Gulf, Red Sea and Indian Ocean and still play a key part in the economy and livelihood of the cities. Dhows are by far the most evocative reminder of bygone days in old Dubai and Abu Dhabi.

APPEARANCE

Dhows are often painted in bright colours, particularly around the raised sterns. They vary in size from 15m to 40m (50–130ft), weighing anything from 30 tonnes to over 500.

CONSTRUCTION

Dhow-building has been a source of astonishment for Europeans and Arabs from the Mediterranean for centuries. Boats are not nailed together but stitched and glued. First, the hull is lined with planks of teak, impregnated with shark oil to prevent rot. Planks are then stitched together edge to edge with coconut twine, and the ribs fitted later – the reverse of the European, frame-first shipbuilding method. A mixture of shark fat and lime is then boiled together to make an efficient, airtight filler, which continues to outperform any modern equivalent. Gaps between the boat's boards are then caulked with the mixture. The main advantage of such a construction is that it proves more supple, lithe and resilient in heavy surf and is less likely than heavier-built ships to be smashed while coming ashore.

PERFORMANCE

The characteristic lateen (triangular) sail allowed boats to sail close to the wind. Dhows attain a maximum speed of about 5 to 6 knots. Most dhows are also fitted with engines.

NAVIGATION

Taking advantage of seasonal winds, sailors voyaged to foreign ports during the winter and returned home in the summer. The Arabs also developed the *kamal*, a remarkable navigational device that allowed them to determine latitude by gauging the height of the Pole Star above the horizon. Navigation was always without the use of maps.

WHERE TO SEE DHOWS

DUBAI

Dhow Construction Yard
Just south of Al Garhoud Bridge, Jaddaf; times vary, usually Sat–Thur 8am–6pm; map p.135 C1
Here dhow makers still fashion the ancient vessels by using techniques and

Left: dhow cruise ship.

Sat–Thur 9am–7pm, Fri 4–9pm; map p.134 C1
With around a dozen dhows, Al Boom is the largest dhow operator on the Creek, offering a variety of cruises and prices, including lunch and late-night trips on the water.

Al Mansour Dhow
Radisson SAS Hotel, Baniyas Road; tel: 04-222 7171; www.radissonblu.com; daily boarding 8pm; map p.131 C2
Offering an Arabic and international buffet to the sound of a strumming *oud* (a kind of Arab lute), cruises aboard the Al Mansour are popular.

ABU DHABI

Al Dhafra
Off 31st Street, near Fish Market, Al Meena; tel: 02-673 2266; www.aldhafra.net; map p.137 E4
Fitted with a *majlis* (a traditional Arabic sitting room) on the upper deck, and laying on an extensive international buffet (including Arab dishes), the Dhafra offers nightly dinner cruises on the Corniche from 8.30 to 10.30pm.

DHOW RACING
Dubai
Various locations; Oct–May
Racing takes place in the winter, culminating in May in the **Sur Bin Naa'ir Dhow Race**, in which boats re-enact the old pearling tradition of racing home to much-missed families.

Abu Dhabi
Various locations off Abu Dhabi Corniche; Sept–Apr; www.emirates-heritageclub.com
Don't miss the chance to see dozens of dhows racing off the coast.

Most Arabian seaman in pre-modern times spent days and nights exposed to the elements, often in conditions of considerable hardship. Even a partial deck or a cabin was a luxury.
The boat was essentially a cargo-carrying tub, which also required constant maintenance. Crew and passengers accommodated themselves as best they could on top of the cargo, and ablutions were carried out in a precarious box slung out over the side of the boat.

ools passed down from generation to generation.

Dhow Wharfage
Near the Hilton Dubai Creek, the Creek, Deira; map p.131 D1
Come at dusk to watch the dhows returning to port and to see them unpack their cargo. If you can find a captain that speaks English, they're often happy to talk about their boats and can usually tell a tale or two about their adventures.

Left: awaiting the next voyage.

ABU DHABI

Dhow Building Yard
In front of Marina Sports Club, Khor Bateen, Al Bateen; times vary, usually Sat–Thur 8am–6pm; map p.136 A2
At the yard, you can see the master craftsmen at work with tools that have remained almost unchanged for millennia.

Dhow Harbour
West of Fish Market, Al Meena; map p.137 E3
Lying just behind the Fish Market, the dhow harbour makes a great place for a sunset stroll. Bring your camera and watch the weather-beaten and hard-working crews unpack their cargo.

DHOW CRUISES
A cruise aboard a dhow provides not just a memorable evening, but an entirely different view of the cities. It's a must.

DUBAI

Al Boom Tourist Village
Near Al Garhoud Bridge, tel: 04-324 3000; www.alboom.ae;

Environment

Dubai and Abu Dhabi boast many things; among them unfortunately is one of the world's worst environmental records, and one of the largest ecological footprints on the planet. With the cities' lightning-quick development – from Third World to First World in about 25 years – it's the environment that's paid the price. Furthermore, with its rather nineties culture of must-have-at-any-price (including ecological) consumerism, the cities are beginning to look rather out of tune with the times, despite the obsession with technology and 'progress'. But signs of environmental stirrings are showing.

WILDLIFE

Rapid urbanisation and uncontrolled hunting have taken a heavy toll on Dubai and Abu Dhabi's wildlife. Where once oryxes, leopards, cheetahs, aardwolves, striped hyenas and caracals roamed in abundance, all of these species are now either extinct in the region or on the brink of extinction. Efforts to conserve the beautiful, indigenous Arabian oryx have met with some success. **Sir Bani Yas island** in Abu Dhabi is the site of a much-praised breeding programme for endangered wildlife.

Lying on a migratory crossroads between Europe, Africa and Asia, and with an abundance of man-made water sources, Dubai and Abu Dhabi attract nearly 350 migratory species. One good place to see birds, including greater flamingos, is at the **Ras Al Khor Wildlife Sanctuary** in Dubai.

The other principal place to see wildlife is underwater. Dubai and Abu Dhabi's waters boast over 350 species of fish, including several species of shark and dolphin, and their coral reefs are home to a good variety of tropical fish, turtles and rays. Hawksbill and Green turtles (the Arabian Sea is famous for the latter) used to nest on beaches in Dubai. No longer. Very occasionally seen in the shallow coastal waters around Abu Dhabi's island is the famously elusive and herbivorous dugong, or sea cow, which sailors once mistook for mermaids.

ENVIRONMENTAL THREATS

Dredging

Typically, if you don't have something in Dubai or Abu Dhabi, you buy it or you make it. Even land. Unable to purchase more land, Dubai is instead fashioning it from sand dredged from the seabed. On the surface this results in spectacular, palm-shaped island projects. Underwater, it's another story. Environmentalists claim that the seabed is suffering irreparable damage and that the coral reefs are suffocating from the silt. The developers claim to be consulting environmental agencies and that fish are returning to the sites; it remains to be seen what long-term damage the coasts will sustain.

Left: Greater flamingos at Ras Al Khor Wildlife Sanctuary.

Left: Dubai darkens its icons to support Earth Hour.

as Burj Al Taqa (Energy Tower), 55° Dubai (the world's first perpetually rotating tower) and the Iris Tower will incorporate solar panels, wind turbines, water recycling equipment and self-air-conditioning systems into their designs. Abu Dhabi's Masdar City, meanwhile, will become the world's very first carbon-neutral city. The latest in solar panels will meet the energy needs of the population in its entirely.

Energy Consumption

Dubai and Abu Dhabi gobble more energy per inhabitant than any nation on Earth, even America. The city has no usable water and among the lowest rainfall of anywhere in the world. So, to feed the city's 24-hour sprinkler systems, satisfy the luxury hotels' vast consumption needs, and to irrigate such projects as the almost perfectly pristine golf courses (which are reputed to require 18 million litres/4 million gallons of water per course per day), the cities are obliged effectively to suck up their own sea.

The vast desalination plants used to do this cost millions of dollars to operate – costing more even than petrol to produce, and in the process belching tons of carbon dioxide into the sky. Hence Dubai and Abu Dhabi's good citizens have the largest ecological footprint of any people on Earth.

REFORMS
Eco-friendly Buildings

Fortunately, things are changing. Many of the tabled new buildings, such

Manacling Mother Nature

Many visitors are struck by a certain incongruity in the cities. Desiring to build the biggest and the best, to boast – and even outdo – any and every attraction found anywhere else in the world, the city has created some truly bizarre 'experiences'. Ski Dubai is in essence an Alp-sized freezer maintained at a steady -2°C (28°F), whilst the torpid air outside can touch 43°C (109°F) in July. At Dubai Mall, among the world's top five largest shopping malls, you can browse live penguins and seals after the shoe-shopping and Starbucks; and at the newest arrival on the hotel block, the Atlantis, there is an aquarium so large it once contained its very own whale shark. Its 'Swim with Dolphins' experience is permanent, since they're penned and specifically trained to kiss and hug the tourists who pay through the nose to meet them.

GOVERNMENTAL MEASURES

Stung by international criticism, embarrassed by local environmental campaigns and genuinely interested in advice from their expat environmental consultants, the authorities of both cities are beginning to take environmental issues seriously.

Both cities' governments have pledged to cut water consumption by more than half by 2015, and reduce fuel consumption by at least a quarter.

Other efforts include city-wide campaigns to educate citizens in environmental awareness (particularly in schools), and above all to value and preserve water.

Right: solar parking meter.

51

Essentials

The biggest question facing many visitors is when to go. During the summer months (May–Sept), temperatures in the UAE can touch 48°C (118°F). With high humidity to boot (up to 95 percent), the cities can seem like saunas, and even the sea provides little relief. Most locals spend their summers in the mall. Nonetheless, the summer's a great time to scoop up serious bargains of up to 60 percent or more at top hotels and shops. The ideal time to visit is probably Nov–Apr, when temperatures hover just above 30°C (86°F) and there's plenty happening in the cities, including some of their most famous festivals.

BUSINESS HOURS

The UAE's working week is from Sunday to Thursday; many companies also work on Saturday. Friday is the equivalent of the West's Sunday, with most places closed, at least until after prayer around 3 or 4pm. Private companies work from 9am to 5pm, some government offices from 7 or 8am to 2pm. Most malls open daily from 10am to 10pm (to midnight on Thursday to Saturday).

Above: escaping the heat.

Left: Friday prayers punctuate the work week, closing most shops and businesses.

CUSTOMS

Duty-free entitlement per person is: 4 litres (1 gallon) of spirits (or two cartons of beer), 400 cigarettes, 50 cigars and 500g (17 oz) of tobacco. Beyond the usual prohibited items are pornography, pork products and unstrung pearls. Note that visitors carrying even traces of drugs face immediate imprisonment – famously demonstrated in 2008 when a visitor was jailed for four years when found to be carrying a grain of cannabis on the sole of his shoe. Certain medication like Codeine is also banned so check before travelling.

ELECTRICITY

Local supply is 220/240 volts AC, 50Hz. Most sockets are designed for British-style, 13-amp, three-pin plugs.

EMBASSIES/ CONSULATES

Australia: 04-508 7100 (Dubai); 02-401 7500 (Abu Dhabi)
Ireland: 04-331 4213 (Dubai); none in Abu Dhabi

Left: interior of Wafi Shopping Mall, Dubai.

friendly for fear of being shut down. Gay websites are the best sources of information, though note that these are blocked by web censors inside the UAE itself.

HEALTH

Visitors to the UAE face few health risks, bar perhaps the heat and the roads. Be sure to bring plenty of sun cream; in the hot summer months, drink plenty of water, and drive (and walk) defensively on the roads.

Both Dubai and Abu Dhabi boast well-equipped private and public hospitals (and pharmacies). Free emergency health care is provided to expats and visitors in certain government hospitals (including those listed below). For non-emergency treatment or private health care

Wi-Fi hotspots are multiplying in both cities. Many coffee shop outlets (including Starbucks), shopping malls and some restaurants and cafés provide hotspots for Etisalat (one of the UAE's two telecommunications companies), which can be accessed via a pre-paid card (usually available from the locale itself or computer stores). For a current list of hotspots see: www.etisalat.ae. Many malls, some hotels and cafés offer their own wireless services free to customers making a purchase.

New Zealand: 04-332 7031 (Dubai); none in Abu Dhabi
UK: 04-309 4444 (Dubai); 02-610 1100 (Abu Dhabi);
US: 04-309 4000 (Dubai); 02-414 2200 (Abu Dhabi)

EMERGENCY NUMBERS
Ambulance: 998
Fire: 997
Police: 999

ETIQUETTE
There is a definite expectation that visitors will show respect for the local culture and dress modestly. This generally means covering legs to the knee and covering shoulders when away from the beach or poolside. Fines or warnings can be given to anyone who dresses inappropriately. Couples should also be careful how they behave; public displays of affections are frowned upon and kissing in public is not allowed. Drinking and driving is strictly forbidden as is all drug use. Swearing is also not acceptable.

GAY & LESBIAN
Under UAE law, homosexual acts are illegal. Though there's certainly a scene in both cities and particularly Dubai (where recently a mass gay wedding took place clandestinely, though it was soon raided by police), no venue would advertise itself as gay-

Right: the shopping begins (and ends) at Dubai airport's duty free.

53

Generally considered the UAE's best **English-language newspaper** is *The National* (www.thenational.ae) printed in Abu Dhabi and the only paper that compares to decent Western broadsheets for its quality of writing. Other major papers available in both cities (but printed in Dubai) include: *Gulf News* (www.gulfnews.com), *Emirates Today*, *Gulf Today*, *Khaleej Times* and the tabloid-style *Xpress* and *7Days*. International newspapers are widely available, though often censored by the authorities. The UK's *The Times* now prints an international daily edition in Dubai; the *Financial Times* does a Middle East edition.

(which can be very costly), ensure you have adequate insurance (which should also cover you for any holiday activities such as scuba-diving, water sports or quad biking – check the coverage carefully). On-call doctors are available in many hotels.

DUBAI

Dubai Hospital
Off Al Khaleej Road, Al Baraha; tel: 04-219 5000; www.dohms.gov.ae; map p.131 D4

Rashid Hospital
Oud Metha Road, near Al Maktoum Bridge, Bur Dubai; tel: 04-219 2000; www.dohms.gov.ae; map p.134 A3

Latifa Hospital (Maternity and Paediatric)
Off Al Wasl Road, Oud Metha; tel: 04-219 3000; map p.134 A1

ABU DHABI

Sheikh Khalifa Medical City
24th Street, off 11th Street, Al Karama; tel: 02-819 0000; www.skmc.ae; map p.137 C2

INFORMATION
For tourism information, contact the following authorities:

DUBAI

Department of Tourism & Commerce Marketing
9th, 8th and Ground Floor, Al Fattan Plaza, Airport Road

Deira; tel: 04-282 1111; www.dubaitourism.ae

ABU DHABI

Abu Dhabi Tourism Authority
Al Salam Street, Bain Al Jessrain; tel: 02-444 0444; www.abudhabitourism.ae
In Dubai, information centres are also found in the airport arrivals lounge and dotted around the city. Most hotels in both cities can provide basic town maps; good bookshops sell more detailed maps of both the cities and the emirates.

INTERNET ACCESS
Dubai and Abu Dhabi are very into the net. All the larger hotels offer in-room access (many wireless), though it's not cheap. Many hotels offer business centres, sometimes on a complimentary basis. Independent internet cafés, found in both cites, are reasonably priced (from around Dh5 per hour). Be aware that any sites considered to be unsuitable are censored and it will be impossible to access them.

MONEY
The UAE's currency is the dirham (Dh), which is divided into 100 fils. Currently pegged to the US dollar, you can check current rates at: www.xe.com.
ATMS are found at banks, the larger hotels and shopping malls and Visa, MasterCard and American Express are widely accepted. The cities' moneychangers sometimes offer better rates than the banks.

Left: international finance, Dubai's one true essential.

Right: local gossip mags.
Below right: service standards
are impeccably high.

POST
Emirates Post (Empost) is
the national postal com-
pany. Postal facilities can
be found in all the major
malls. Mail takes between
seven to 10 days to
Europe and the US, up to
16 days to Australia.

SMOKING
In January 2008, smoking
was banned in all enclosed
public spaces except bars
and clubs, unless the
venue contained a spe-
cially adapted area (few
places do). Smokers con-
travening regulations risk
fines of Dh500–1000.
Smoking is permitted out-
side and on terraces.

TELEPHONE
The UAE's telecommunica-
tion system is modern and
reliable. Etisalat (www.eti-
salat.com) and Du
(www.du.ae) are the sole,
largely government-owned
telecom companies. Both
companies offer competi-
tively priced, temporarily-
enabled SIM cards
designed for visitors which
include some free phone
credit in the package.
Phonecards for public tele-
phones are also widely
available
   The UAE's international
dialing code is +971. Reach
the operator on 100; Direc-
tory Enquiries: 181.

TIME
The UAE is GMT plus four
hours; there is no seasonal
adjustment.

TIPPING
Most 'tourist' hotels and
restaurants automatically

include a 15 percent service charge in bills; if not,
10 percent is the norm. As
the low-paid waiters rarely
see the included tip, it's
kind to leave something
extra if the service has
been good. Taxi fares are
usually rounded up, and
valets or others performing
small services usually
receive between Dh2–5.

VISA INFORMATION
Visa regulations change
regularly; always check the
latest information with the

UAE embassy in your
home country. In general,
tourist visas valid for 60
days are available free
upon arrival at major
points of entry (airports
and ports) to citizens of
most developed countries,
bar Israel. For other countries, visas must be
arranged through a local
sponsor. Passports must
be valid for six months
from the date of entry.
Beware overstaying your
visa; fines of over Dh100
per day are imposed.

55

Fashion

While you can find an impressive number and range of international designers in Dubai and Abu Dhabi's shops, Emirati designers are only slowly beginning to emerge. More and more home-grown boutiques are beginning to open, and in 2008 Abu Dhabi hosted its very first international Fashion Week. Top designer names are usually found in the cities' five-star hotels or upmarket malls; a few independents are opening in Dubai's Jumeira district. For the budget-conscious, a trawl of the streets in Dubai's Karama district or Abu Dhabi's Al Markaziyah, or even the cities' hypermarkets can yield terrific bargains.

ACCESSORIES

DUBAI

Azza Fahmy Jewellery
Bloomingdales, Dubai Mall; tel: 04-350 5333; Sun– Wed 10am–10pm, Thur–Sat 10am–midnight
The jewellery of renowned Egyptian designer Azza Fahmy is inspired by everyday things such as birds and palm trees to motifs from Arabic proverbs or poetry. Highly original and beautifully crafted, pieces make eye-catching accessories.

Karama Shopping Centre
18B Street, Karama, Bur Dubai; Sat–Thur 9am–10.30pm, Fri 9am–11am, 4–10.30pm; map 133 D2
For copies of designer handbags and accessories, Karama in Bur

> ### Malls
> Dubai continues to play one-upmanship with itself and has unveiled plans for a new Nakheel Mall on the Palm, expected to open in 2016.

Dubai is the best bet. Most expats have their favourite shop, often with a back room bursting to the seams with items many would mistake for the real deal. Shopping here can be quite an experience.

ABU DHABI

Damas
Abu Dhabi Mall, 10th Street; tel: 02-645 4864; www.damasjewel.com; Sat–Thur 10am– 10pm, Fri 2–10pm; map p.137 E2
Like a kind of high-quality, high-class Ratner's, Damas is an institution in the Middle East. Gold jewellery is its speciality: there's a huge selection, and prices are competitive.

BARGAINS, OUTLETS & SECOND–HAND

DUBAI

Priceless
Al Maktoum Street; tel: 04-221 5444; Sat–Thur 10am–10pm, Fri 2–10pm
A well-kept expat secret, the well-named Priceless sells the former stock of famous London fashion

store Harvey Nichols, at dazzling discounts of up to 85 percent. Names range from Alberta Ferretti to Alice + Olivia and Jimmy Choo, and include men's and women's clothes and shoes.

Reem's Closet
Mazaya Centre, Al Wasl; tel: 04-343 9553; www.reems closet.com
Almost unknown in Dubai, Reem's Closet sells second-hand clothing – only it's designer. A catch-all for expats bored of posh party numbers, it's great for snapping up top names in clothing, shoes and handbags at bargain prices (though prices have increased recently). Names include Dior, Vuitton and Hermès.

Sell Consignment Shop
Ground Floor, Sultan Business Centre, near Lamcy Plaza; tel: 04-334 2494; Sat–Thur noon–9pm; map p.133 D2
Also selling second-hand designer clothes, shoes and accessories from Prada to Anna Sui, the

Left: traditional hairdress and modern fashion.

Five Green

Behind Aroma Garden Café, Oud Metha Road; tel: 04-336 4100; www.fivegreen.com; Sat–Thur 10am–10pm, Fri 4–10pm; map p.133 E3
A boutique-cum-art space-cum-music store, Five Green is the most original and interesting boutique in town, and is also one of the few places to find clothes by Dubai designers.

Ginger & Lace

Ibn Battuta Mall; tel: 04-368 5109; www.gingerandlace. com; Sun–Wed 10am–10pm, Thur–Sat 10am–midnight
Ginger & Lace is firmly established on the city's fashion scene. Stocking nearly 130 international brands in icing-pink surroundings, it offers fashionable, original but wearable clothes, shoes and accessories in a wide range of materials and styles.

Praias

Mall of the Emirates, Sheikh Zayed Road; tel: 04-341 1167; Mon–Wed, Sun 10am–midnight, Thur–Sat noon–10pm; map p.14; Metro: Mall of the Emirates
If you've forgotten your cozzie but still want to look the part on the beach, Praias stocks some snazzy swimwear.

range is good and stock is regularly replenished.

ABU DHABI

Hamdan Centre

Near Novotel Centre Hotel, Sheikh Hamdan bin Mohamed Street; tel: 02-632 8555
An old fave of expats, the Hamdan sells clothes and shoes at remarkably reasonable prices, though don't come here for *haute couture*.

BOUTIQUES

DUBAI

Ayesha Depala

The Village, Jumeira Road; tel: 04-344 5378; Sat–Thur 10am–10pm
The first Indian designer to boast a shop in Dubai's Saks Fifth Avenue, Ayesha Depala is a star on Dubai's fashion scene. Her feminine clothes range from cardigans to evening dresses.

Bambah

142 Jumeira Road, opposite Dubai Zoo; www.bambah.com; tel: 050-6741754; daily 10am–10pm
A rare vintage store in a gorgeous villa which sells dresses, blouses and accessories from the 30s through to the 80s.

Boom & Mellow

Mall of the Emirates, Sheikh Zayed Road; tel: 04-341 3993; Mon–Wed, Sun 9.30am– 10pm, Thur–Sat 9.30am– midnight
The first top-end accessories boutique in town, Boom aims to be definitive too: it's crammed to the rafters with original, high-quality accessories of all types, including beach dresses. Perfect for outfit-hunters planning to party.

Right: fashions collide at Ibn Battuta shopping mall.

The **shopping mall** is an institution in the UAE. A modern-day solution to a climate which, for almost half the year, is too hot to stop, the shopping mall plays a vital commercial and economic role. For the locals (Emiratis as well as expats), the malls serve a vital social function too. It is here that friends hook up, families spend quality time together (particularly after the Friday prayer), and young people date. Business is also conducted here and deals sealed. As malls multiply, competition between them increases, and they battle to keep their customers. You can now not just shop, eat and drink in malls, but also go to the cinema and theatre, visit funfairs and amusement arcades; ski, ice skate, visit an aquarium, an underwater zoo – every year the experiences become ever more diverse and perverse. But for a glimpse into the cities' soul, it's unmissable.
See also Shopping, p.116.

S*uce
The Village Mall, Jumeira Road; tel: 04-344 7270; www.shopat sauce.com; Sat–Thur 10am–10pm, Fri 4.30–10pm
One of the city's hippest boutiques, S*uce stocks an original, very eclectic and carefully selected range of funky clothing and accessories by established European names as well as young international designers, ranging from Toast handbags to Citizens of Humanity jeans.

DEPARTMENT STORES

DUBAI

Bloomingdales
Dubai Mall; tel: 04-350 5333; Sun–Wed 10am–10pm, Thur–Sat 10am–midnight; map p.12

The New York store has been brought to Dubai; the first Bloomingdales to open outside the US. It offers three floors of fashion and accessories as well as a personal shopping service,

Boutique 1
The Walk JBR, Dubai Marina; tel: 04-425 7599; daily 10am–midnight
With nearly 175 brands within its walls offering everything from street hip to classic and funky by both established and new talent, Boutique 1 is considered *the* one-stop shop by Dubai's fashionistas, both for men and women. There is another branch of Boutique 1 at Mall of the Emirates (tel: 04-395 1200).

Harvey Nichols
Mall of the Emirates, Sheikh Zayed Road; tel: 04-409 8888; www.harveynichols.com; Mon–Wed, Sun 10am–10pm, Thur–Sat 10am–midnight
The famous high-end London fashion store recently opened its doors in Dubai with its charac-

Left: Mercato Mall.

teristically comprehensive range of international designers and excellent accessories section.

Saks Fifth Avenue
Burjuman Centre, Trade Centre Road; tel: 04-351 5551; www.saksfifthavenue.com; Sat–Thur 10am–10pm, Fri 2–11pm; map p.130 C1; Metro: Khalid Bin Al Waleed
Offering the signature Saks top-end selection spread over two floors, designers include Manolo Blahnik, Prada and Missoni.

ABU DHABI

Splash
Centre Point, next to Marina Mall; tel: 02-681 6063; www.splashfashions.com; Sun–Wed 10am–10pm, Thur–Sat 10am–midnight; map p.136 B3
One of the very few homegrown fashion retail brands in the region, it's also the fastest-growing, offering trendy clothing adapted to local tastes at excellent prices. At 2,500 sq m (28,000 sq ft), this is its biggest outlet to date.

LINGERIE

DUBAI

Nayomi
Mercato Mall, Jumeira Road; tel: 04-344 9120; www.nayomi.com.sa; Sat–Thur 10am–10pm, Fri 2–10pm
The largest retailer of lingerie and nightwear in the Gulf, Nayomi prides itself on creating feminine designs 'with an oriental twist'. Other items include slippers and eau de toilette in ornate bottles.

ABU DHABI

Nayomi
Abu Dhabi Mall, 10th Street;

tel: 02-645 4741; www.nayomi.com.sa; Sat–Thur 10am–10pm, Fri 2–10pm; map p.137 E2
The regional favourite stocks its signature collection of quality but reasonably priced lingerie and nightwear in a range of styles, materials and colours.

SHOES

DUBAI

International Aladdin Shoes

Directly in front of abra station, Dubai Old Souk, Bur Dubai; daily 8am–10pm; map p.130 B2
Though little more than a stall, Aladdin sees a lively tourism trade for its delightful decorated slippers (some pointy-toed), which come in all colours and sizes.

Kurt Geiger

Deira City Centre, Level 2, Baniyas Road; tel: 04-294 3395; Sun–Wed 10am–10pm; Thur–Sat 10am–midnight; map p. 131 E1; Metro: Deira City Centre
American-owned Kurt Geiger sells designer brands of shoes and can be found at the following malls as well; Dubai Festival Centre, Dubai Mall, Marina Mall and Mirdif City Centre.

Vincci

Bur Juman Centre, Trade Centre Road; tel: 04-351 7246; Sat–Thur 10am–10pm, Fri 2–10pm
The popular Malaysian brand's mantra is to offer a huge variety of fashionable, quality footwear at affordable prices, with new designs launched every season. It's consid-

ered one of the city's best women's shoe shops.

ABU DHABI

Shoe Mart

Madinat Zayed Shopping Centre; tel: 02-634 6461; Sat–Thur 10am–10pm, Fri 2–10pm; map p.137 D2
A firm favourite locally for offering fashionable shoes at inexpensive prices, Shoe Mart is also known for its wide range: from street-pacing comfies to clubbing killers.

TAILOR–MADE

Hundreds of Asian tailors make their home in both cities. Many are highly skilled and can create clothing from sketches or photos, or copy existing items. The backstreets of Dubai's Bur Dubai or Abu Dhabi's Hamdan Street are good hunting-grounds, but try to get a recommendation, and agree a price before commissioning. The following are have big local followings:

DUBAI

Dream Girl Tailors

Opposite Emirates Bank International, near Satwa round about; tel: 04-349 5445; Sat–Thur 10am- 1.30pm, 4–9.30pm, Fri 6–8pm; map p.132 A2

As in other Gulf countries, Emirati women in public don an *abeyya* (black covering) over their clothes and a *shayla* (black headscarf) to cover their hair (an Arab proverb claims 'a woman's beauty is her hair'). The more conservative women additionally wear a black or sometimes gold *burka* which partly, or wholly, conceals their face. Conversely, Emirati men, like many of their Gulf neighbours, don a *dishdasha* (a long shirt-dress), a *gutra* (head cloth that's worn in a distinctive Emirati way), and an *agal* (black head rope that, in the days of Bedouin living in the desert, was used to hobble camels). Few fashion opportunities there, you might think. In recent years, however, the *abeyyas* of younger women have been sprouting all kinds of adornments, from coloured embroidery, sequins and beads to leopard-print linings, feathers and even little gold charms. Men, on the other hand, have been spied in sharply cut *dishdashas* coloured all sorts of fashionable hues.

ABU DHABI

Al Esayi Textile

Abu Dhabi Mall, adjacent to Beach Rotana Hotel; tel: 02-645 0313; Sat–Thur 10am–10pm, Fri 2–10pm; map p.137 E2

Right: a selection of colourful fabrics.

Festivals and Events

In the ongoing bid to get tourism to gush like an oil well, Abu Dhabi and Dubai have conjured up several major cultural and sporting events. Constructing state-of-the-art, no-expense-spared venues, and luring the world's top entertainers and sporting stars with megabucks, these events have become major engagements on the world's sporting and cultural calendar. If you're keen to catch an event, and take advantage of the lavish entertainment laid on, here's a list of the principal ones.

JANUARY

Dubai Marathon

www.dubaimarathon.org
With its million-dollar prize money, the marathon lures some of the swiftest-footed stars in the world, including Ethiopian winner Lelisa Desisa, who was the victorious man in 2013.

Abu Dhabi Golf Championship

Abu Dhabi Golf Club by Sheraton; www.abudhabi golfchampionship.com
Dangling a 2 million-dollar prize, and with the official sanction of the European Tour, Abu Dhabi attracts some of the world's top players, who fight fiercely to raise the 'Falcon Trophy'.

FEBRUARY

Dubai Desert Classic

Jan/Feb; Emirates Golf Club, Dubai Marina; www.dubai desertclassic.com
Soon to be eclipsed by the new Dubai World Championship, the DDC remains a central event in the PGA European Tour. With its US$2.4 million prize money, it attracts all the top names, including Stephen Gallacher who won in 2013.

Dubai Duty Free Tennis Open

Late Feb/early Mar, two weeks; Dubai Tennis Stadium, Garhoud; www.dubaitennis championships.com
Part of the prestigious ATP (Association of Tennis Professionals) tournament for men and WTA (Women's Tennis Association) tournament for women, these singles matches attract all the top-ranking seeds, male and female.

MARCH

Dubai World Cup

Medhan Racetrack, Nad al Sheba, off Al Ain Road; www.dubaiworldcup.com
Totalling US$6 million in prize money, the cup is the richest horse race in the world, as well as the top event in the city's social calendar.

Taste of Dubai Festival

Media City; www.tasteof dubaifestival.com
For several days, this foodie festival celebrates the art of cooking with live demonstrations, chefs from the Dubai restaurant scene and a market featuring local suppliers.

Abu Dhabi Music & Arts Festival

Left: the Dubai Open.

Left: the Global Village.

Hollywood, Bollywood and the Middle East. Both the glam red-carpet events and most screenings sell tickets to the public.

Global Village

Dec–Feb, 4pm–midnight, three months; Dubailand, Emirates Road; www.globalvillage.ae
Coinciding with the DSF, the Global Village is an enormous funfair and a gigantic shopping opportunity. It's a big hit with families.

Mar–Apr; various venues; two weeks; www.abudhabi festival.ae
Staging an eclectic mix of ballet, concerts, recitals and exhibitions, the festival features over 500 artists. Acts in the past have ranged from the Globe Theatre, to Mariinsky Ballet and Placido Domingo.

APRIL
Abu Dhabi Desert Challenge

Oct/Nov; four days; www.abu dhabidesertchallenge.com
Starting in Abu Dhabi and heading into the Liwa Desert and the Moreeb area of the Empty Quarter, the race is one of the foremost motorsport events of the region.

NOVEMBER
Dubai Rugby Sevens

Late Nov/early Dec; three days; The Sevens, on the Al Ain Road; Dubai Exiles Club; www.dubai rugby7s.com
A new stadium called The Sevens (which also hosts concerts) shows you how seriously Dubai takes this

sport. Comprising part of the IRB World Seven Series tournament, the event is a charming combination of 16 high-profile international squads, mixed with some very enthusiastic local amateurs.

DP World Tour Championship, Dubai

The Earth Golf Course, Jumeirah Golf Estates, Dubai; www.dpworldtourchampion ship.com
This golf tournament is played on 'The Earth', a course designed by Greg Norman with a prize fund of US$8 million.

Abu Dhabi Grand Prix

Yas Marina Circuit; www.formula1.com
This world-class event is held at the iconic Yas Marina Circuit in November.

DECEMBER
Dubai International Film Festival (DIFF)

Madinat Jumeirah; Jumeira Road; www.dubaifilmfest.com
The festival attracts filmmakers and stars from

The Islamic holy month of **Ramadan** is the most important event in the Islamic calendar, observed by all Muslims around the world. During this time, Muslims are required to fast (nothing must pass their lips) between dawn to dusk. For many Muslims, the month represents an opportunity to cleanse themselves physically, mentally and spiritually. Some non-Muslim visitors prefer to stay away since they also are required to observe the fast in public. Many of the large hotels still offer food during the day from some of its restaurants by curtaining off the eating areas. It is expected that non-Muslims will show respect by not eating in their car or taxi; some forget they're still on show. Additionally, nightclubs close down and alcohol is only served at some bars after nightfall. On the other hand, the *iftar* (breaking of the fast) celebrations at dusk have a unique atmosphere and community spirit about them and visitors are warmly invited to join. It can make for an extremely rewarding and illuminating visit. **Eid** is the joyful holiday which follows Ramadam and is a time of feasting and celebrating with family.

Food and Drink

In Dubai you can find any food you want. Thanks to the cities' enormous expat population (which comprises over 150 nationalities), you can find eateries that range from Ethiopian and Bangladeshi to Azerbaijani and Philippine. In fact almost the only cuisine you can't find is Emirati. Locals tend to eat at home, and no Emirati woman would risk being seen at an Emirati restaurant lest her cooking skills be questioned. If you're lucky enough to be offered an invitation to eat with Emiratis, don't miss it. The hospitality extended to a guest is legendary. *See also Bars and Cafés, p.30–7,* and *Restaurants, p.102–13.*

ARABIC CUISINE

While modern Arabic cuisine derives from a whole host of influences including Egyptian, Iranian and Moroccan, the term is most commonly used to refer to Lebanese food.

MEZZE

Mezze – small dishes and dips – are the Middle East's equivalent of tapas. Staple *mezze* scooped up with flat Arabic bread are hummus (a chickpea paste with olive oil, garlic and lemon juice), *tabbouleh* (a parsley and cracked wheat salad with tomato), *fattoush* (a finely chopped tomato, cucumber and lettuce salad), *mutabel* (similar to hummus but made with smoked aubergine) and *fattayer* (pastries filled with cheese and spinach). Though usually followed by a main, *mezze* can be enjoyed as a satisfying meal in themselves.

MAINS

Main courses usually consist of charcoal-grilled lamb, chicken or fish – served either whole or in large pieces, or as a sheesh kebab, served with a salad. Other mains include *kibbeh*, minced meat patties made with bulgur wheat and spices, and for a special celebration, *khouzi,* in which a whole lamb is served on a bed of rice mixed with nuts and sometimes fruit such as raisins or apricots.

DESSERTS

Arabic desserts typically feature nuts, syrup and fresh cream. Classic and popular puddings include *Umm Ali* ('Mother of Ali'), a very rich bread-and-butter pudding with sultanas and coconut, topped with nuts, as well as *kashta*, clotted cream topped with pistachio, pine seeds and honey. Pastries are also popular, such as the Turkish *baklava* (filo pastry layered with nuts and syrup).

FAST FOOD

Arabic fast food consists usually either of *shawarma* (lamb or chicken cooked on a vertical spit and served with garlic paste in Arabic bread) or *falafel* (mashed chickpeas, sesame seeds and spices rolled into a patty and deep-fried).

DRINKS

Traditional Arabian coffee *(kahwa)* is flavoured with cardamom and served in small, handleless cups. In restaurants, Turkish coffee – with heavy sediment at the bottom – is more commonly served. If you don't drink your coffee sweet, ask for 'medium sweet' *(wasat)* or 'without sugar' *(bidoon sukkar)*. Arabic-style tea is also served sweet, without milk and often flavoured with cardamom or fresh mint.

TABOOS

Muslims, including Emiratis, traditionally refrain from drinking alcohol. In Dubai and Abu Dhabi, visitors are permitted to drink alcohol, but it is only served in licensed venues

Left and below: grilled meats, whether served in a fine restaurant or on the street, play an important part in Emerati cuisine.

chios, lemons, limes (from Iran) and dried fruits. Reflecting Asian influences, dishes today are often served biriani-style with rice, or as kebabs.

Other mains include: *matchbous*, spiced lamb with rice; *harees*, slow-cooked barley and lamb; *fareed*, a meat-and-vegetable stew poured over flat bread; *ouzi* (goat slow-roasted on a bed of rice, egg and onion); and *thareed* (a casserole made with lamb, vegetables and bread). Flavourings include cumin, cardamom and coriander.

For something approximating a traditional Emirati restaurant serving traditional food (albeit more Lebanese than Emirati), try **Bastakia Nights** (Bastakia, Bur Dubai; tel: 04-353 7772; daily 12.30–11.30pm; map p.130 B2). Set in a traditional courtyard-style house in the historical quarter of Bastakia, it certainly plays the *1,001 Nights* fantasy card shamelessly, but the lanterns, candlelight and

> The annual food festival Taste of Dubai (www.tasteofdubai festival.com) is held at Media City and offers visitors a chance to taste food from the city's top restaurants.

EMIRATI CUISINE
Emirati food derives largely from two main sources. The first is the simple Bedu fare that was the mainstay during erstwhile days in the desert. This consisted largely of lamb, chicken and sometimes fish, stewed in pots. The second influence comes from the UAE's merchant past, which exposed the region to new ingredients and cooking influences. Spices such as saffron, turmeric, cinnamon and fenugreek began to be adopted, as well as almonds and pista-

attached to hotels (in other words hotel bars and restaurants), as well as some of the larger leisure clubs (such as golf and sports clubs). Restaurants outside hotels are not allowed to serve alcohol.

Pork is also taboo in Islam. Muslims are not permitted to prepare, serve or eat pork. However pork products are widely available in upmarket restaurants and the menu will specify if a dish contains pork or alcohol. In restaurants, it must be prepared, cooked and stored in a separate area (so that it does contaminate other food). Pork is sold in some supermarkets, Spinneys stocking the best selection, but it is in a separate section marked 'for Non-Muslims'.

One of the very few plants adapted to the arid Emirati climate is the **date palm**. Cultivated for millennia, it is the world's oldest harvested fruit. Nearly all parts of a date palm were traditionally used: the fruit for eating and cooking, the trunk for ceiling beams and the fronds to make roofs, basket ware, hats and prayer mats. Until around 50 years ago, the Bedu survived for days in the desert on a diet of just dates and camel's milk. Old habits die hard: Emiratis still love their dates. They are offered to guests (as they are in many Emirati hotels) and taken for sustenance during long journeys (including the *Haj*, the Muslim pilgrimage). During Ramadan, dates (eaten in even numbers only) are used to break the fast. Dates are also brought to friends in hospital, and Emirati mothers eat dates mixed with herbs after childbirth. Modern analysis shows that, along with a high energy content, dates also contain high levels of fibre, vitamins and minerals (including potassium, iron and magnesium).

courtyard soon melt the most cynical of hearts.

FOOD SHOPS

DUBAI

Chocoa

Across the road from Mall of the Emirates, off Sheikh Zayed Road; tel: 04-340 9092; Mon, Tue, Sat, Sun 10am–11pm, Wed–Fri 10am–midnight; map p.14; Metro: Mall of the Emirates

Chocolate heaven *à l'orientale*, Chocoa sells an enticing selection of chocolates and goodies of all types, ranging from high-quality dried-fruit to dates dipped in chocolate and tiny syrup-

soaked pastries. It's a great place to buy gifts for sweet-toothed friends or family back home.

Organic Foods & Café

Dubai Mall, Downtown Burj Dubai, off Ras Al Khor Road; tel: 04- 434 0577; www.organic foodsandcafe.com; daily 8am–10pm; map p.12; Metro: Burj Khalifa/ Dubai Mall

Dubai's first organic supermarket is the place to shop is you're into healthy, ethical eating. It's also excellent for people who may have food allergies or be on special diets. The attached café serves delicious fruit juices and teas. There is also a branch on Sheikh Zayed Road next to the Oasis Center.

Patchi

Souk Madinat Jumeirah, Jumeira Road; tel: 04-368 6101; www.patchi.com; daily 10am–11pm

A branch of the highly successful Lebanese chocolate chain Patchi, the shop sells its signature stuff: decent-quality chocolate turned into beautiful gifts, including truffles served on silver platters or in crystal dishes. With a choice of over 30 fillings, the pick 'n'

Left: harvesting a date palm.

mix option at the counter can be overwhelming.

Wafi Gourmet

First Floor, Wafi City, Oud Metha; tel: 04-327 9940; Sat–Wed 10am–10pm, Thur–Fri 10am–midnight; map p.135 A1

A feast for the eyes Wafi Gourmet is a large deli where you can buy beautifully presented Arabic pastries and sweets, dates as well as an excellent selection of mezze dishes which you can take away. It has a terrace restaurant attached. A branch is also open at Festival Centre.

ABU DHABI

Patchi

Marina Mall, Breakwater; 02-681 7554; www.patchi.com; daily 10am–10pm; map p.136 B3

Offering its clever combination of quality chocolates beautifully packaged, Patchi remains one of the region's most popular sweet shops.

FISH MARKETS

DUBAI

Deira Fish Market

Opposite Hyatt Regency Dubai, near Shindagha Tunnel; Sat–Thur 9am–1pm, 4–10pm, Fri 4–10pm; map p.130 B3

Even if you're not buying, the market's well worth a visit for the buzz and the banter between buyers and sellers, as well as the extensive range of fish and seafood. If you are buying, there's a section to the side which will clean the fish for you. For the best atmosphere (and freshest

Right: exotic fruit and fish on sale at local souks.

fish), come either first thing in the morning or last thing at night.

ABU DHABI

Fish Souk
Meena Street, Al Meena; Sat–Thur 4.30am–6pm, Fri 4–10pm; map p.137 E3

A trip to inspect the daily catch at the city's fish market is well worthwhile, with fishy produce ranging from octopus and shark to squid and ray, with every shape, colour and size of fish in between, including the ubiquitous hammour, a member of the grouper family and much loved locally.

FOOD MARKETS

DUBAI

Fruit & Vegetable Souk
Next to the Fish Market (see above); Sat–Thur 9am–1pm, 4–10pm, Fri 4–10pm; map p.130 B3

With a great selection of fruit from all across the world – some you may never have seen before – the Fruit Market makes a colourful, interesting and fun stop. Vendors will offer you samples to taste and

---

The Coffee Ritual

Throughout the Emirates, elaborate ceremony surrounds the serving of coffee. If offered coffee in office, homes or even hotels, it is polite to accept it. To refuse is to reject an important gesture of welcome and hospitality, and you risk offending your host. Arabic coffee is usually poured from an ornate, long-spouted pot known as a *dalla* into tiny handleless cups. Cups should be accepted with your right hand only. It's considered polite to drink at least three cups (the third is traditionally considered to bestow a blessing). More may be impolite; just follow your host's lead. To indicate that you've had sufficient, swivel the cup slightly between fingers and thumb. Your cup will be removed.

---

are happy to chat about the provenance of their goods. After the Fish Market, the smell of peaches and honey makes a welcome relief.

ABU DHABI

Fruit & Vegetable Souk
Meena Street, Al Meena; Sat–Thur 9am– 6pm, Fri 4–10pm; map p.137 E3

Boasting the freshest fruit and veg in the city, with the widest selection and at the best prices, this is a great place to come if you're craving a fruit fix. Produce is sold by the kilo; vendors are happy to sell one or two pieces, and will often let you try produce first too.

SPICE MARKETS

Spice Souk
Off Old Baladiya Street, Deira; generally Sat–Thur 8am–1pm, 4–9pm; map p.130 B2

The Spice Souk is one of the very few places where you're instantly transported to times gone by. The souk here has existed for centuries, though sadly it's much diminished from its former days, as urban development, modern supermarkets and changing customs have slowly strangled it. If the vendors aren't too busy, they're usually happy to pass on the century-old secrets of herbal remedies and potions: rose water for a healthy heart, pomegranate peelings for an upset stomach and fenugreek for flatulence!

History

c.5000 BC
Stone Age settlements are established on the Arabian Gulf coast and in the Hajar Mountains.

2700–2000 BC
A Bronze Age settlement is founded at Al Sufouh, Dubai.

1st century BC
An Iron Age village is established at Al Ghusais, Dubai.

4th century AD
Christianity arrives in Bet Mazunaye (modern-day UAE and northern Oman).

6th century
The Sassanids establish a trading post in Jumeira. Aramaic becomes the region's lingua franca.

c.632–5
The Battle of Dibba marks the dawn of the Islamic era on the Arabian peninsula. Arabic replaces Aramaic.

16th century
Portuguese imperialists recognise the strategic importance of Arabia's coast en route to India's riches.

1580
The earliest surviving written reference to 'Dibei' is made by Venetian jeweller Gasparo Balbi.

1793
Dubai, a fishing and pearling village of 1,200 people, becomes a dependency of Abu Dhabi.

1822
A British treaty with Mohammed Bin Hazza is the first formal recognition that Dubai is a separate entity to more powerful neighbours, Abu Dhabi and Sharjah.

1833
Maktoum Bin Buti Al Maktoum and 800 members of the Bani Yas tribe arrive in Shindagha from Abu Dhabi, marking the beginning of Maktoum rule.

1841
The Maktoums extend their influence across the creek, from Bur Dubai to Deira.

1853
The Perpetual Treaty of Maritime Truce between Britain and local sheikhs safeguards British sea trade with India. The region becomes known as the 'Trucial Coast'.

1894
Sheikh Maktoum Bin Hasher uses tax concessions to encourage foreign merchants to settle in Dubai.

1902
Increased customs duties in the Persian port of Lingah provoke the migration of foreign traders to Dubai's free-trade zone.

Below: an early image of dhows in Dubai harbour, dating from 1834.

1929

Wall Street Crash causes pearl prices to plummet. The newly introduced Japanese cultured pearl sounds the industry's death knell and plunges Dubai into economic depression.

1958

Sheikh Rashid Bin Saeed Al Maktoum, the 'father of modern Dubai', becomes ruler.

1966

Oil is discovered in Dubai. Exports begin within three years.

1971

The United Arab Emirates (UAE) is established, with Abu Dhabi ruler Sheikh Zayed Bin Sultan Al Nahyan as president and Dubai's Sheikh Rashid as vice president.

1983

Dubai Duty Free is established at Dubai International Airport.

1985

Dubai-based airline Emirates is founded.

1990

Sheikh Rashid dies. His son Sheikh Maktoum Bin Rashid Al Maktoum succeeds.

1996

The Dubai Strategic Plan forecasts the expiration of oil by 2010; plans are made to diversify the economy. The Dubai World Cup, the world's richest horse race, is inaugurated, as is Dubai' first Shopping Festival.

2001

Following the tourism boom, work begins on the Palm Jumeira and the Palm Jebel Ali, two man-made islands.

2002

Leading property developers announce 100 percent freehold ownership for non-nationals, unleashing a construction boom.

2004

Sheikh Zayed, founder and president of the UAE, dies aged 86. His son Sheikh Khalifa becomes president.

2006

Sheikh Maktoum dies aged 62. His brother Sheikh Mohammed succeeds him as vice president and prime minister of the UAE and ruler of Dubai. Population of Dubai surpasses 1.4 million.

2007

Burj Dubai becomes the world's tallest building on 21 July. Thousands of construction workers strike for two days in October demanding better working conditions and increased pay.

2008

Sheikh Mohammed names his son, Hamdan bin Mohammed bin Rashid Al Maktoum, as Dubai Emirate's crown prince and probable successor.

2009

The Dubai Financial Market loses 48 percent of its value. On 22 February, the central bank buys US$10 billion-worth of Dubai's bonds – oil-rich Abu Dhabi effectively bails out Dubai. In March Sheikh Khalifa, UAE president, pledges federal financial support for the UAE's troubled banks and state companies.

2013

The tallest hotel in the world opens on Sheikh Zayed Road, the JW Marriott Marquis Hotel, and with it a sense of Dubai's recovery and ambition to keep breaking records.

Hotels

No two cities in the world offer such a diversity of upper-range accommodation as Dubai and Abu Dhabi. Despite efforts to launch budget accommodation in the cities, the UAE is still perceived as a luxury destination, but as the plethora of families filling the four- and five-stars will attest, there are few places where such comfort can be had at such prices. With hotels competing fiercely to offer the finest facilities and with the cities' licensing laws limiting the selling of alcohol to bars, clubs and restaurants within hotels, many visitors end up spending much of their time in the confines of their hotel. For many, the hotel even ends up forming a highlight of their holiday.

DUBAI: DEIRA

Ahmedia Heritage Guest House

Next to Al Hamadiya School, Al Hamadiya Street; tel: 04-225 0085; www.ahmedia guesthouse.com; $; map p.130 B2; Metro Al Ras

Ahmedia Heritage Guest House is well named: the small hotel occupies a traditional, 150-year-old courtyard house, with rooms giving onto it. Rooms have private bathroom, satellite TV and are spotlessly clean and furnished with lovely, carved wooden furniture. The hotel provides two things so often lacking in Dubai: history and atmosphere. Note that alcohol is not served, and the hotel's proximity to the mosque makes for an early call in the morning.

Price categories are for a standard double room, excluding breakfast, in the high season:
$ Dh500 or less
$$ Dh500–1,000
$$$ Dh1,000–1,500
$$$$ Dh1,500 or more

Above: a cocktail with a view at the Rotana.

Al Bustan Rotana Hotel

Casablanca Road; tel: 04-282 0000; www.rotana.com; $$$; map p.135 D3

Situated less than five-minutes' drive from the airport, the Al-Bustan is a popular business hotel and meeting place, boasting one of the biggest conference rooms in Dubai. It prides itself on an 'Arab welcome', efficient management and friendly and attentive service. Facilities include an attractive pool area, a gym, squash court, three tennis courts, and some first-rate restaurants including the Dubai outlets of the famous Blue Elephant (Thai), Beni Hana (Japanese) and Rodeo Grill (steakhouse) restaurants. Newly refurbished, rooms are spruce, well equipped, decent-sized and comfortable.

Carlton Tower Hotel

Baniyas Street; tel: 04-222 7111; www.carltontower.net; $$; map p.130 C2

It may be looking its age a little, but with a convenient central location, a rooftop pool, a couple of restaurants plus a pub,

Left: Le Méridien's pool, *see p.78*.

spending what you save on rates on taxi fares.

Hilton Dubai Creek

Baniyas Road; tel: 04-227 1111; www.hiltonworldresorts. com; $$$; map p.131 D1
Conceived by international architect Carlos Ott, the Hilton Dubai Creek is designer inside and out. All in wood and chrome, glass and granite, it's chic and understated, but the views of the Creek from the floor-to-ceiling windows of some its rooms and the rooftop pool are stunning. Rooms are well equipped, service is spot-on, and the hotel is home to several good restaurants and bars, including Table 9.
SEE ALSO RESTAURANTS, P.104

InterContinental

Dubai Festival City; Near Garhoud Bridge; tel: 04-701 1111; www.intercontinental. com/dubai; $$$$; map p.135 D1
The new and comfortable Intercontie boasts among its boons proximity to the airport, a key position at the

---

Hotels often make good spots for seeking **taxis**. Generally there are two options: the city taxis that queue up hoping to catch a customer, and the hotel's dedicated taxis parked outside. The latter are more expensive and can cost anything from 15 percent to 50 percent more depending on the length of the journey and the duration (beware the traffic at peak hours). Though doormen are trained to point you towards the latter, an 'I think I'll take a city taxi' usually does the trick.

(the only one in town) is more up market than most: facilities include a pool, tennis court, gym, spa, sauna, Jacuzzi and billiards room. Offering dorm rooms, singles, doubles and even family rooms, it's clean, well run and well maintained – and is also popular. Reservations are essential. Note that it is a little way out of town. Unless you use the buses (Nos 3, 13, 17 and 31 connect the place with the centre), you may end up

and rooms with pretty views (those of the Creek are extra), the hotel represents good value for money. It's a popular choice with package tours, so be sure to reserve well in advance.

Dubai Youth Hostel

39 Al Nahda Road, near Al Mulla Plaza; tel: 04-298 8161; www.uaeyha.com; $
Even Dubai's youth hostel

Right: Hilton Dubai Creek.

Left: Park Hyatt Dubai.
Right: Four Points by Sheraton. Far right: Mövenpick Hotel Bur Dubai.

Dubai and Abu Dhabi's hotels, which must meet municipal regulations and inspections, are generally kept pretty spick and span, even the cheapies. In the lower category ($), the great majority of hotels have private bathrooms and air conditioning. What makes them 'budget' is usually their size: the room and its bathroom. Mid-range rooms ($$) usually come with satellite TV and a minibar as standard. The four ($$$) and five ($$$$) stars are usually spacious, well furnished and well equipped, and keen competition between them sees them fairly regularly renovated. However, few five-stars genuinely meet the high international standards required of this class in terms of top-notch service and attention to detail.

Luxurious they may be, but staff rarely receive the rigorous training they do in other countries. As for the self-awarded seven stars (Burj Al Arab in Dubai and the Emirates Palace in Abu Dhabi), like many things in the cities, that's mere hype and hyperbole.

heart of the up-and-coming (and fast-developing) Festival Centre, a prime waterfront location on the Creek, two major golf courses on its doorstep, and some top-rated restaurants including the famous **Reflets**, recently voted the city's best French restaurant.
SEE ALSO RESTAURANTS, P.103

Park Hyatt Dubai

Next to Dubai Creek Golf & Yacht Club, off Al Garhoud Road; tel: 04-602 1234; www.dubai.park.hyatt. com; $$$$; map p.134 C3
Moorish in design, layout and decoration, the lavish Dubai Creek's main perks are its prime position on the waterfront – with all rooms boasting a balcony or terrace with Creek views, and its peaceful setting in the grounds of the **Golf and Yacht Club**. Facilities include one of the city's best spas – **Amara** – a 25m (82ft) pool and excellent restaurants.
SEE ALSO PAMPERING, P.96; SPORTS, P.118

BUR DUBAI
Arabian Courtyard

Al Fahidi Street; tel: 04-351 9111; www.arabiancourtyard. com; $$; map p.130 B2
Set round the back of the Dubai Museum, the Arabian Courtyard lies in the centre of Old Dubai close

to its sights. A good number of the 173 rooms have views across to the Creek, and its facilities include a small pool and gym, a Wellness centre, a reasonable northern Indian restaurant and a British-themed pub, the Sherlock Holmes. The Arabian-themed rooms are comfortable, well furnished and good value.

Dhow Palace Hotel

Kuwait St; tel: 04-359 9992; www.dhowpalacedubai.com; $$$; map p.132 C4
With a striking, modern facade modelled like a dhow, the nautical theme is stretched a boat too far with the dhow fountain, swirling-sea carpet and doormen dressed as sailors. But the architecture is impressive and the five star-rated rooms are generously sized. With a rooftop pool (albeit modest), health club, spa, a good selection of restaurants, a bar and business centre, this new arrival is well priced in its category.

Four Points by Sheraton

Khalid bin Walid Street; tel: 04-397 7444; www. fourpoints.com/burdubai; $$; map p.130 B1; Metro: Khalid Bin Al Waleed
Part of the new trend of up

Price categories are for a standard double room, excluding breakfast, in the high season:

$	Dh500 or less
$$	Dh500–1,000
$$$	Dh1,000–1,500
$$$$	Dh1,500 or more

market internationals targeting businessmen on a budget, the Four Points lacks the luxury and fancy flourishes of its five-star sisters, but is still comfortable, well run and well equipped, with gym, small pool, and good restaurants and pub. It offers good value.

Golden Sands Hotel Apartments
Off Mankhool Road; tel: 04-355 5553; www.goldensands dubai.com; $$; map p.133 C4
Offering self-catering, serviced and decent-sized apartments of one, three and four bedrooms, the Golden Sands is a good option if you're in Dubai for a couple of weeks or more. Facilities include a gym and squash courts, and in the apartments there's a small kitchen and washing machine.

Mövenpick Hotel Bur Dubai
19th Street; tel: 04-336 6000; www.moevenpick-hotels.com; $$; map p.133 E2
After setting eyes on the slightly kitsch and gaudy lobby, rooms seem rather staid by comparison, but they're comfortable and well furnished, and many

have city views. In keeping with the Mövenpick chain's reputation, the hotel food is half-decent, the service is Swiss-efficient and the hotel is well run. The hotel is also home to some popular restaurants and bars, and on the rooftop there's an attractive pool area and running track. The Friday brunch here is recommended.

Raffles Dubai
Off Sheikh Rashid Road,Wafi; tel: 04-324 8888; www.raffles.com/dubai; $$$$; map p.134 A1; Metro Healthcare City
New five-star on the scene – and icon on the block – is the unmissable, 19-storey, pyramid-shaped Raffles. Aspiring hard to the standards of its famous Singaporean sister, it's luxurious in materials, decor, facilities and service. Among the facilities offered are butler service, a Bose CD system, a 24-hour on-call doctor, library and 1-hectare (2½-acre) Botanical Garden. It's also home to some of the city's best restaurants.

XVA Art Hotel
Al Seef Road, near Al Fahidi Roundabout, Bastakia; tel: 04-

353 5383; www.xvahotel.com; $$; map p.130 B2
Lying in the heart of the historical quarter of Bastakia, this guesthouse is a genuine diamond amid the glitz of Dubai. The building, a lovingly restored courtyard house complete with wind-towers, is home to Dubai's first 'art hotel': beside the rooms, there's a well-respected gallery and much-frequented café. It even has its own artists-in-residence who occupy two of the eight boutique-style rooms. Each room varies, some are small and simple, but like the gallery and café, it's the atmosphere and kindred spirit you come for.

DUBAI: JUMEIRA
Burj Al Arab
Jumeira Road; tel: 04-301 7777; www.burj-al-arab.com; $$$$; map p.14
Despite creeping competition from the Burj Khalifa, the Burj Al Arab is still the city's number-one icon, and has become a tourist attraction in its own right. As famous for its astonishing architecture – it is hung, like the sail sheet of the Arab dhow it is supposed to represent, from a giant steel

71

Abu Dhabi and Dubai used to be cheap destinations; now they rate among the most costly cities in the world, particularly – pity the expats – for rented accommodation (where a three-bed flat in the Marina goes for around Dh150,000 a year and a large villa in the gated communities scattered throughout Dubai Dh300,000). Nevertheless, luxury remains more affordable here than in many places, and package deals, seasonal discounts, plus the recent economic downturn and fierce competition between establishments makes bargain-bagging a real possibility. Recently, in an attempt to combat falling tourist numbers, five-star hotels were offering discounts of up to 60 percent in the high season. Good deals can be found during Ramadam, Eid and the hotter summer months.

exoskeleton that's large enough to contain the Eiffel Tower in its entirety – as for its claims to be the world's first and only seven-star hotel. Built on its own island, it also boasts its own helipad, its own fleet of Rolls-Royces, and a staff-to-guest ratio of 6:1. Inside, it's just as startling architecturally. The interior design may not be to everyone's taste (particularly the gratuitous gold gilding and kilometres of Swarovski crystal chandeliers), but it's certainly bold. If you can't reach to the rates, it's well worth breaching the Burj's guests-only entry policy by having a drink in the famous **Skyview Bar**.
SEE ALSO BARS AND CAFÉS, P.33

Right: the Raffles cuts an unmissable profile, *see p.71.*

Capitol Hotel

Al Mina Road, off Mankhool Road, Satwa; tel: 04-346 0111; www.capitol-hotel.com; $$
If you're keen to stay near Jumeira but can't stretch to the five-stars, the large, canary-yellow Capitol is not a bad bet. Its 168 rooms are spacious and perfectly comfortable (with double-glazing to keep out street noise, a minibar and internet access); there are a couple of restaurants and a bar, a small rooftop pool and a diminutive gym.

Jumeirah Beach Hotel

Jumeira Road; tel: 04-348 0000; www.jumeirahbeach hotel.com; $$$$; map p.10
Designed to resemble a cresting wave, the Jumeirah Beach Hotel is another famous and familiar landmark. Despite its iconic credentials, the hotel has become popular with package-deal families, and has a casual, family-orientated environment. Lying near (and with complimentary entry to)

In 2012, 8.8 million visitors over-nighted in one of Dubai's many hotels. Ever ambitious, the government hopes to see that number nearly double (to 15 million) by 2015.

the **Wild Wadi Waterpark**, it also boasts a kids' club, adventure playground and children's pool. Other facilities include tennis courts, water sports, a PADI dive centre and a golf driving range, as well as dozens of restaurants and bars.
SEE ALSO CHILDREN, P.42

Kempinski Hotel

Mall of the Emirates, Al Barsha; tel: 04-341 0000; www. kempinski.com; $$$$; map p.14; Metro: Mall of the Emirates
Offering both shopping and sporting activities par excellence, the Kempinski might make the perfect choice for a couple. Conjoined to one of the world's largest shopping centres, the Mall of the Emirates, it also overlooks **Ski Dubai Snow Park**, the Middle

In a campaign to cast the cities' tourism net still further, Dubai and Abu Dhabi's officials are actively seeking to establish their cities as budget destinations as well as luxury ones. Projects range from budget-class hotels designed for dirham-leery business travellers, to more reasonably priced dining and drinking options. Among the groups joining the budget-hotel bandwagon are: easyHotel (www.easyHotel.com), Ibis (www.ibishotel.com), which plans hotels in Dubai's Barsha district and the Mall of the Emirates, Centro Rotana (www.centrobyrotana.com), Holiday Inn Express (www.hiexpress.com), with hotels opening in Jumeira, Media City, Barsha and Safa, and Sheraton's Four Points (www.FourPoints.com). Rates will start from around Dh340. Though hardly dirt-cheap, it's certainly beats Burj Al Arab at Dh6200 for a king-size. Hotels and their restaurants are increasingly offering dining discounts too, including up to 50 percent for 'early birders' (eating dinner before 8.30pm), as well as offering good-value set menus and brunches. Some hotels are also starting to offer special deals on their spa treatments. Enquire.

East's first 'ski resort', as well as offering a tennis court, gym, spa and pool. It scores high on novelty value too: you can rent a 'ski chalet' with views of the 'slopes'.

SEE ALSO CHILDREN, P.41

Mina A'Salam

Al Sufouh Road; tel: 04-366 8888; www.madinatjumeirah.com; $$$$; map p.14
Styling itself on Arabia's old mud-brick architecture, topped with a home-grown wind-tower or two,

the enormous Mina A'Salam and Madinat Jumeira complex is definitely more Disney than history. Nevertheless, the

Price categories are for a standard double room, excluding breakfast, in the high season:	
$	Dh500 or less
$$	Dh500–1,000
$$$	Dh1,000–1,500
$$$$	Dh1,500 or more

complex of Venice-like canals that cut through the complex, the lovely views over them and the sea, the deluxe fabrics and furnishings *à l'orientale* make it a fun fantasy to visit. Less lush and plush than its brother hotel the Al Qasr in the same complex, the Mina

Above: Burj Al Arab, *see p.71.*

73

still offers the same high-level comfort and fabulous facilities, including no fewer than 45 restaurants, bars and cafés to choose from.

Al Qasr

Al Sufouh Road; tel: 04-366 8888; www.madinat jumeirah.com; $$$$; map p.14
Intended as the 'Jewel in the crown' of the Madinat Jumeirah hotel complex, the Al-Qasr is an Orientalist's fantasy. Designed like the summer retreat of an Arabian prince, it's all lavish materials – plump cushions, decorative drapes and swathes of richly coloured fabric meet Moorish decor – lanterns, *mousharibiyya* (perforated wooden screens) and *zellij* (decorated tiles) with gorgeous vistas thrown in at every opportunity. Al Qasr is also known for its top-notch butler service, its spa (one of the best in the city), the picture-perfect beach, and the rather romantic *abras* (Dubai Creek's water taxis) which ferry you about the Madinat Jumeira complex via the network of purpose-built canals.

Price categories are for a standard double room, excluding breakfast, in the high season:	
$	Dh500 or less
$$	Dh500–1,000
$$$	Dh1,000–1,500
$$$$	Dh1,500 or more

DUBAI: SHEIKH ZAYED ROAD
The Address

Burj Dubai Boulevard, Downtown Burj Dubai; tel: 04-436 8888; www.theaddress.com; $$$$; map p.12
The Address is an award-winning luxury five-star which backs onto Dubai Mall and dominates the downtown Burj Dubai block. Forming the flagship of several other future hotels, its target is the business traveller the DBD is increasingly attracting. Standing 63 storeys high, its super-sleek, chic and state-of-the-art rooms have startling views of the Burj Dubai and cityscape, close proximity to the city's best shops, access to a superb spa, spectacular infinity pool, a business centre, library and seven of the city's top restaurants and bars.

Armani Hotel

Burj Khalifa, Downtown Burj Dubai; tel: 04-888 3888; www.dubaiarmanihotels.com; $$$$; map p.12
Understated elegance is quite hard to come by in Dubai. The Armani hotel design is as sophisticated as Giorgio Armani's fashion brand; the hotel's interiors are cool, immaculate and desireable. Everything including the staff is beautiful. It's the only hotel inside the Burj Khalifa and it seems far removed from the bustling world which surrounds it. There are 160 rooms and suites, a spa and some excellent restaurants.

Dusit Thani

Sheikh Zayed Road; tel: 04-343 3333; www.dusit.com; $$$
One of the most striking buildings on the Sheikh Zayed strip, the Thani is designed to represent the traditional Thai gesture of two hands joined together in greeting. It's emblematic of the hotel, which is renowned for assiduous service and traditional Thai hospitality. Rooms are well designed and restful; many boast striking city views.

To get the best out of your stay in Dubai, it's worth thinking about the main purpose of your trip: business, beach, family hol, shopping, sightseeing or sport? In a nutshell, Deira is great for local colour (in the form of souks, ethnic restaurants and cafés), but bad for locating taxis. Hotel-wise, it offers everything from backstreet cheapies to Creekside luxuries. Bur Dubai is best for sightseeing and also ethnic eateries and is unbeatable for Old Dubai atmosphere. Hotels range from backstreet low-budgets to excellent mid-rangers and even an all-too-rare boutique hotel. Sheikh Zayed Road, the new financial and geographical hub, is best for business, shopaholics and modern-architecture aficionados. Taxis are easy to come by (though rush hour traffic is notorious), and hotels and restaurants range from middling to super-luxurious. Jumeira and Dubai Marina are best for beach, sport and activity fans, as well as families, and the archetypal Dubai atmosphere of glitz and glamour. Hotels range from a rare B&B option to family-friendly complexes and top-of-the-range luxury. Inland from Dubai Marina are some of the city's best shopping malls.

Above: the sumptuous interior of Al Qasr.

There's also an attractive rooftop pool, gym, small spa and an excellent Thai restaurant and a bar. For the location, it's good value.

Emirates Towers

Sheikh Zayed Road; tel: 04-330 0000; www.jumeirahemirates towers.com; $$$$; map p.12; Metro: Emirates Towers

Left: Jumeirah Beach Hotel, *see p.72.*

Winner of *Business Traveller UK*'s Best Business Hotel in the Middle East 2011 award, the Emirates Towers is Dubai's corporate hotspot and an icon in itself. Standing 305m (1,000ft) high (in the smaller of the two towers), it's among the world's highest hotels, and its startling city views are one of its major selling-points. Slick, sleek, and well fitted out, the hotel also prides itself on its service. Facilities include a large pool, gym, spa and even its own little mall, **The Boulevard**, itself home to an excellent selection of cafés, bars and restaurants.
SEE ALSO SHOPPING, P.117

Fairmont Dubai

Sheikh Zayed Road; tel: 04-332 5555; www.fairmont.com; $$$$; map p.132 B1
Designed to evoke a stylised wind-tower, the Fairmont is another iconic landmark, particularly at night when the tops of its towers change colour. Inside, all in chrome and glass, it's similarly striking. Befitting the reputation of this blue-blooded five-star,

rooms are suitably spacious, well equipped and very comfortable. There's also a lovely rooftop pool, a top-notch spa and some outstanding restaurants.

Ibis World Trade Centre

Behind World Trade Centre, Sheikh Zayed Road; tel: 04-332 4444; www.ibishotel.com; $; map p.132 C1; Metro: Trade Centre
Forfeiting the frills and flourishes of the four- and five-stars, the Ibis serves up simple, rather small but perfectly smart and comfortable rooms at unbeatable prices. Facilities are limited to restaurants and bars, but guests can use the pool, gym and spa of the nearby Novotel for a small fee. Popular with dirham-conscious convention-goers, you'll need to book well ahead, but it's one of Dubai's bargains.

Al Manzil Hotel

Old Town, Downtown Burj Dubai; tel: 04-428 5888; www.almanzilhotel.ae; $$
A good deal on the four-star scene is the chic and well-designed Al Manzil. The decor is modern

75

meets oriental, with pistachio-painted rooms furnished with gold blinds, old photos and white leather chairs; baths float seductively in the middle. From the balconies and rooftop pool there are impressive views of the city skyline, but the bar-cum-restaurant in the courtyard can preclude an early night.

The H Hotel Dubai

Trade Centre Roundabout, 1 Sheikh Zayed Road; tel: 04-501 8888; www.h-hotel.com; $$$$; map p.132 B1
Positioned right opposite the World Trade Centre is the H, formerly Monarch. With its target customers – well-heeled businessmen – literally within its ranges, it offers top-notch rooms and suites that are overtly executive in form and function. Modern-Orientalist in decor, all rooms have a designated office area, as well as dramatic floor-to-ceiling city views. Facilities include a business centre, health club, one of the city's sprucest spas – the **Mandara** – a decent-sized pool and a collection of reputable restaurants and bars.
SEE ALSO PAMPERING, P.97

Al Murooj Rotana Hotel

Al Saffa Street, off Sheikh Zayed Road; tel: 04-321 1111; www.rotana.com; $$$$
Imposing, palatial in size and surrounded by a sort of moat, Al Murooj is fortunately less pretentious than it looks. Spacious and comfortable rooms in bashful browns are designed to appeal to

Price categories are for a standard double room, excluding breakfast, in the high season:
$ Dh500 or less
$$ Dh500–1,000
$$$ Dh1,000–1,500
$$$$ Dh1,500 or more

Business Bay guests. Facilities include a business centre, a fun pool area with a kind of cascade, a gym and a spa. It's also home to the lively Double Decker bar, and several restaurants that are well liked locally.

The Palace

Old Town, Mohammed Bin Rashid Boulevard; Downtown Burj Dubai; tel: 04-428 7888; www.theaddress.com; $$$$
Designed like a traditional *qasr* (fort or palace), this new luxury hotel is well-named, inside and out. All 242 of its rooms boast butler service, state-of-the-art gadgetry, the finest fabrics and materials and stunning views of the Burj which soars skyward above it. The hotel is also home to several fine-dining

restaurants, a lavish spa and a magnificent palm-studded pool. In 2011, the Palace won Dubai's Leading City Resort in the World Travel Awards.

Shangri-La Hotel Dubai

Sheikh Zayed Road; tel: 04-343 8888; www.shangri-la.com; $$$$
Unmistakable for its tall twin towers, the Shangri-La also stands out for its supremely chic and understated comfort, superior service and beautifully designed and furnished rooms. Other boons include stunning views over both the city and the sea, some of the city's best restaurants, two large pools (including one the rooftop), and a giant gym. For some, it's Dubai's No.1.

Towers Rotana Hotel

Sheikh Zayed Road; tel: 04-343 8000; www.rotana.com; $$
Centrally located, well managed and welcoming, the Towers Rotana offers one of the best deals on the strip. Though it for-

Right: the Thai-inspired Dusit Thani, *see p.74*.

Above: the sleek, modern and unmissable Emirates Towers, *see p. 75.*

goes the fancy flourishes and studied style of its more sophisticated (and expensive) neighbours, it still offers comfortable and spacious rooms and good facilities, including a pleasant rooftop pool, gym and spa, and a couple of top-class city restaurants and bars, including **Teatro**.

SEE ALSO RESTAURANTS, P.109

DUBAI MARINA
Atlantis
Palm Jumeira; tel: 04-426 0000; www.atlantisthepalm.com; $$$$; map p.14

Much anticipated, the new Atlantis has now opened its doors (and 1,500 rooms) to guests. Though vast and impressive for its sheer scale and ambition (including a metro-style train that spans the sea, connecting the Palm Jumeira island to the mainland), it may not be everyone's cup of tea. The themed decor (inspired by the legend of the lost kingdom of Atlantis) is Liberace-lavish and looks a little like Santa's Grotto gone nautical. Lying at the

hotel's epicentre is an aquarium so vast that it contained – controversially – its very own whale shark, along with 65,000 fellow marine creatures. Accommodation ranges from spacious and comfortable rooms with sea views to spectacular suites walled by the aquarium. Atlantis's biggest asset is its facili-

Dubai and Abu Dhabi's hotel rates fluctuate dramatically, depending on the season, time of year (over European holidays, local festivals, etc), and the deal (booking through websites or travel agents almost always buys better rates than rack rates published by the hotels). Be sure to shop around.

To bag a bargain, consider coming during the low season (the stifling summer months of June to August, when rates can drop by up to 75 percent. The peak season is from October to April (and particularly November to February). Shop around, always request the 'best rate' and enquire after any current 'special deals'. Even the five-stars run these.

ties for kids, including a proactive Kids' Club; Club Rush, designed for teenagers, offering everything from iMacs and video games to live DJs, movies and a Chill Lounge; **Aquaventure**, a 16-hectare (40-acre) waterpark; the **Lost Chambers**, an aquarium-cum-theme park; a 700m (2,300ft)-long beach, and **Dolphin Bay** – equally divisive – in which the 'swim-with-dolphin' experience is permanent since they're penned. Among the famous chefs overseeing the hotels restaurants are Michel Rostang, Giorgio Locatelli, Santi Santamaria and Matsuhisa Nobu.

SEE ALSO CHILDREN, P.40

Grosvenor House
West Marina Beach, Al Sufouh Road, Dubai Marina; tel: 04-399 8888; www.grosvenorhouse-dubai.com; $$$$; map p.14

Rising to 45 floors, the aristocratic Grosvenor (it was the first hotel at the Marina) boasts fabulous views in all directions: the city skyline, the Palm

77

Dubai and Abu Dhabi's hotels have the highest occupancy rate in the world, with an annual average of 86 percent (98 to 99 percent or higher during the winter). During the peak season, you'll need to reserve well in advance. Be sure also to bring confirmation of your booking with you and let the hotel know what time you plan to checkin; overbooked hotels and administrative errors are not uncommon. Check-in time is usually between 1pm and 3pm on the day of arrival. Checkout is usually between 10am and noon. Check that rates are all-inclusive too. Hotels charge 20 percent tax, and ten percent municipal tax plus ten percent service. Upon arrival, hotels usually ask you to leave a credit-card authorisation of about Dh500 per night to cover extras.

Jumeira, the Marina and New Dubai. Rooms are slick, well furnished and well equipped, but the hotel prides itself particularly on its service and facilities, which include the fashionable **Buddha Bar** and **Bar 44**, as well as the **Rhodes Mezzanine** restaurant. The beach and pool feel slightly less exclusive, since guests share that of Le Royal Meridien Beach Resort across the road.

SEE ALSO BARS AND CAFÉS, P.35; RESTAURANTS, P.110

Le Meridien Mina Seyahi Beach Resort & Marina

Al Sufouh Road; tel: 04-399 3333; www.lemeridien-minaseyahi.com; $$$$; map p.14

With one of the longest strips of beach in Dubai (850m/2,788ft), Le Meridien is a popular choice

for sun-seekers, watersport enthusiasts and families, and all three groups are well catered to. It's recently been refurbished. The hotel is also home to the **Barasti Bar**, a very popular local nightspot, as well as some decent restaurants.

SEE ALSO BARS AND CAFÉS, P.35

One&Only Royal Mirage

Al Sufouh Road; tel: 04-399 9999; www.royalmirage.one andonlyresorts.com; $$$$; map p.14

Though the name's trite, the sentiment's sure: the One&Only is in its own class when it comes to understated style, sophistication and refinement. Comprising three hotels in one, the Palace, the Arabian Court and the Residence & Spa, it offers a style (from Orientalist fantasy to more low-key luxury) to suit your mood and adds to that great facilities, including an outstanding spa, an impressive pool, palm-shaded gardens, a

Right: the enormous Atlantis resort plays with themes from the lost city, *see p.77.*

1km (⅔ mile)-long strip of private beach and some of the city's best bars and restaurants. It's also considered one of Dubai's most romantic beach getaways.

Westin Dubai Mina Seyahi Beach Resort & Marina

Al Sufouh Road; tel: 04-399 4141; www.westinmina seyahi.com; $$$$; map p.14

Sharing facilities with Le Meridien Mina Seyahi *(see left),* the new Westin also offers sand, sea and water sports, but in rather more upmarket surroundings. The building is designed like an Arabian *qasr* (palace) gone local, complete with the obligatory wind-towers, but rooms are stylish, modern, well equipped and very comfortable, and many have balconies with sea views. It lies next to the Yacht Club, has pleasant grounds and excellent facilities.

ABU DHABI: CORNICHE
Al Diar Regency

Mina Road, East Corniche; tel: 02-676 5000; www.aldiar hotels.com; $$; map p.137 E3

A good choice for dirham-thrifty business travellers, the Al Diar is located within walking distance of the Business District, boasts a business centre, and a choice of several restaurants and bars. Though rooms are nothing fancy, they're clean

Left: the twin towers of the Shangri-La Hotel Dubai, *see p.76.*

and perfectly comfortable, and all have kitchenettes and balconies with a choice of either city or sea views.

Emirates Palace

West Corniche, tel: 02-690 9000; www.emiratespalace.com; $$$$; map p.136 A3
Built as a kind of riposte to Dubai's Burj Al Arab, the Emirates Palace also lays claims to a 'seven stars' classification, and insists on a rating as a palace rather than a hotel. With its size, grandeur and opulence, palatial it is, though seven-star sadly it is not. Nevertheless, guests are offered every creature comfort, from an initial welcome cocktail and personal check-in service, to

24-hour, on-call butlers and a pillow 'menu', as well as high-tech gadgetry, and great facilities. These include an array of some of the city's finest restaurants, 1.3kms (¾ miles) of whiter-than-white sandy beach, a couple of pools, a luxurious spa, and a private water park. If your dirhams don't bend to a bed here, non-guests are welcome to come for tea, drinks or dinner.

Grand Continental Flamingo Hotel

Hamdan Street, East Corniche; tel: 02-690 4000; www.gcfhotel.net; $$; map p.137 D3
Close to the Corniche, the Financial and Commercial districts, the Grand Continental feels like it's in the thick of things. Rooms are spacious, comfortable and quite well furnished and many have excellent city views. With good facilities to boot, including a decent gym, several restaurants, bars and a nightclub, it represents

some of the best value for money in the city.

Hilton International Abu Dhabi

Corniche Road West; tel: 02 681 1900; www.hilton.com; $$$–$$$$; map p.136 B3
Situated a cab ride from the Financial District, near to the Marina Mall, the Corniche and the beach, the Hilton International has it all, including its own beach club that offers water-sport facilities and a fine, private beach. It is also home to some of the city's most popular bars and restaurants, a luxury spa and health club. Rooms are well furnished and comfortable, and many boast lovely sea views. It was featured in Condé Nast's list of top ten Middle East hotels.
SEE ALSO PAMPERING, P.97

Note that many hotels provide complimentary airport, beach and mall shuttles buses; it's worth enquiring.

Price categories are for a standard double room, excluding breakfast, in the high season:

$ Dh500 or less
$$ Dh500–1,000
$$$ Dh1,000–1,500
$$$$ Dh1,500 or more

Le Royal Méridien

Khalifa Street; tel: 02-674 2020; www.starwoodhotels.com/lemeridien; $$$$; map p.137 D3

One of the city's top business hotels, Le Royal Méridien continues to please punters with its quality furnishings, elegance and professional service. Rooms are well equipped and most boast gorgeous views over the Corniche and Gulf. The hotel also hosts an excellent range of top-notch restaurants, bars and clubs. Facilities include two pools, a fitness centre and a spa.

Sheraton Abu Dhabi Resort & Towers

Corniche Road East; tel: 02-677 3333; www.sheraton.com/abudhabi; $$$–$$$$; map p.137 E3

Situated on the Corniche close to both the beach and the Business District, the Sheraton is a good choice for business travellers and families as well as those in search of sport or some activities. Apart from modern and well-furnished rooms, added boons include water-sport facilities, an attractive, palm-dotted Corniche area containing several heated outdoor pools (including one for kids), a lagoon and a private beach. There's also a spa, a gym, a wide choice of restaurants and bars

that are popular locally, and a pleasant *shisha* café on the beach.

CENTRAL & SOUTH ABU DHABI
Beach Rotana Hotel & Towers

Tourist Club Area; tel: 02-697 9000; www.rotana.com; $$$$; map p.137 E2

With its good sport and leisure facilities, and its direct access to the Abu Dhabi Mall, the Beach Rotana Hotel may be the perfect choice for a couple or those with a family. Facilities include a PADI dive centre, a private stretch of fine sand, a children's play area, tennis and squash courts, an excellent spa, well-equipped gym and a couple of pools (including a children's one). The hotel also houses some of the city's favourite restaurants and bars. Rooms are comfortable, spacious and stylish and also boast impressive sea views.

Al Maha Arjaan by Rotana Suites

Hamdan Street; tel: 02-610 6666; www.rotana.com; $$; map p.137 D3

If you're in Abu Dhabi for more than a week or two, the Al Maha may be the answer. Located conveniently close to the centre of town as well as the Corniche, it offers serviced studio apartments and suites at excellent prices. Apartments are air-conditioned and contain their own kitchenettes with fridge, microwave, washing machine and dryer, and some boast good views of the city to boot.

Le Méridien

Next to Abu Dhabi Marina, off Sheikh Zayed 1st Street, Tourist Club Area; tel: 02-644 6666; www.lemeridienabudhabi.com; $$$$; map p.137 E3

Recently updated and modernised, Le Méridien is a good choice for both business and leisure travellers, but its biggest boon is the verdant and peaceful 'Méridien Village' lying at its centre, which is home to a good number and variety of popular restaurants and bars where you can eat and drink alfresco. Other facilities include pools for both adults and kids, a private beach, a health club and spa that include a hammam and a nightclub. Rooms have panache and are decorated with paintings by local artists, and the service is attentive. Free internet access.

Left: a pampered bath at Le Royal Méridien. **Right:** a regal view from Shangri-La's infinity pool.

If you plan to stay in Dubai or Abu Dhabi for more than a week or two, an apartment may be the answer. Many of the cities' hotels offer serviced, furnished apartments that can be rented by the day, week or month. Prices start from around Dh650 upwards for a midrange studio apartment, but drop significantly the longer you rent them for. The advantage of these hotel-apartments is that you benefit from the hotel's facilities which often include gym, swimming pool, bar and restaurants. Try the following hotel websites for both Dubai and Abu Dhabi: www.rotana.com, and www.cityseasonsabudhabi.com for Abu Dhabi. Additionally for Dubai try: www.mydubaistay.com.

Shangri-La

Off Al Maqtaa Bridge, Bain Al Jesarain; tel: 02-509 8888; www.shangri-la.com; $$$$

The Shangri-La has jumped to a position near the top of the luxury class, and is often the choice of visiting VIPs and celebs. With its palatial size (214 luxurious guestrooms and suites furnished in neo-Moorish design), systems of winding waterways that weave around the complex, its own souk and a plethora of eating establishments, it seems like Abu Dhabi's answer to the Madinat Jumeira in Dubai. Picturesquely positioned on the edge of the Creek that separates the island of Abu Dhabi from the mainland, it boasts stunning views across the water to the new Grand Mosque. Rooms are sumptuously and stylishly furnished, each with a terrace looking onto the water. Facilities include 1km (⅔ miles) of private beach, a sumptuous spa, five swimming pools, a couple of health clubs, and some of the city's best restaurants and bar. Attached to the hotel is the new **Qaryat Al Beri** souk, with its upmarket shops and itself a good selection of bars and restaurants.

YAS ISLAND
Yas Viceroy

Abu Dhabi, Yas Island; tel: 02-656 0000; www.viceroyhotelsandresorts.com; $$$$

Even if you can't afford to stay here, it's worth checking out the striking exterior of the Yas Viceroy, or Yas Hotel as it is known. It is a relatively new landmark in Abu Dhabi boasting 499 rooms and suites and is an integral part of the Grand Prix track. Built half on land and half on water, it is bowl-shaped and from a distance seems to be draped with chain mail. The result is more stunning than it sounds. Like it or not, Yas Hotel exemplifies Abu Dhabi's quest to produce some of the world's most innovative architecture.

Language

Arabic is the official language of the UAE, though in Dubai and Abu Dhabi you may be lucky to hear it. With just 17 percent of the population comprising native Emiratis, English is the lingua franca. Nevertheless, learning a few words of Arabic is worth the effort if only to practise with the Egyptian hotel staff or Lebanese waiters. Any efforts in Arabic by foreigners – particularly Westerners – is hugely appreciated. If you can muster only one phrase, make it the classic Muslim greeting, *as-salaam alaykum*, which for many Arabs shows not just willing but respect towards their religion and culture.

CONVERSING WITH PEOPLE

Hello (informal) *Marhaba*
Greetings (Lit: Peace be upon you; formal) *As-salaam alaykum*
Greetings to you too (response) *Wa alaykum asalaam*
Pleased to meet you/nice to have met you *Fursa sa'ida*
Goodbye *Ma'as/salama*
Thank you (very much) *Shukran (jazeelan)*
You're welcome *Afwan*
Please *Min fadlak*
Yes *Na'am*
No *La*
How are you? (to a man) *Kef halak?*
How are you? (to a woman) *Kef halik*
My name is... *Ismi...*
I am... *Ana...*
Where are you (m/f) from? *Min wayn inta/inti?*
I am from... *Ana min...*

DIRECTIONS

How do I get to...? *Keef boosal lil...?*
Can you show me the way to...? *Mumkin tdallini ala tareeq lil...?*
How many kilometres? *Kam kilometr?*
To/for *Lil*
Left *Shimaal/yasaar*
Right *Yimeen*
Straight *Sida*
Number *Raqam*
City *Madina*
There *Hina/hinak*
This way *Matn hina*
In front of *Qiddaam*
Near *Gareeb*
Far *Ba'aed*
North *Shimaal*
South *Janub*
East *Sharq*
West *Gharb*

EATING

Restaurant *Al mataam*
May I have the menu? *Ana areed al-kaart?*
Do you have...? *Haal indaak...?*
Does anyone here speak English? *Haal yoogaad ahad yatakaallam ingleezi?*
What do you recommend? *Bi madha tinsahnee?*
Do you have vegetarian dishes? *Haal indaak akl nabati laahm?*
Nothing more, thanks *Kafee mashkur*
Just a small portion *Miqdaar sager*
I'd like the bill, please *Ana areed al-hisaab min fadlak*
Delicious! *Ladheedh!*
That was delicious *Kan al aakl ladheedh*
Toilet *Al hammam*

EMERGENCIES

Help me! *Saa' idoonee!*
I'm ill! *Ana mareed/mareeda (m/f)!*
Call the police! *Itasell bil shurta!*
The doctor *Al tabeeb*
Hospital *Al mustashfa*
Police *Al shurta*
Go away/get lost! *Seer!*
Shame on you (if harassed)! *istiHi a'la Haalak!*

HEALTH

I'm unwell *Ana maareed*
My friend is unwell *Sadeeyee maareed*
I'm allergic... *Andee hasasiyya...*
to antibiotics *min al mudad alhayawee*
to aspirin *min al asbireen*
to nuts *min al mukassarat*
to penicillin *min al bin-isileen*

Arabic has several sounds that do not exist in English, including a rolled 'r' (as in Spanish), a 'kh' which is pronounced like the 'ch' in Scottish 'loch', an 'H' pronounced like an out take of breath. a 'dh' sounded like 'th' as in 'this', a 'gh' pronounced like the French 'r', and the letters 'S', 'D', 'T' and 'TH', which are pronounced much more emphatically than their equivalents in English. A few sounds are particularly difficult for non-Semitic language-speakers, includlng 'q', which is strongly guttural, the glottal stop, and the ' ('ayn) which has often been described as the sound of someone being strangled!

I want... *Ana areed...*
Antiseptic *Mutahhir*
Chemist/pharmacy *Al sayidaliyya*
Condoms *Kaboot*
I am/I have... *Ana...*
Diarrhoea *Is-haal*
Fever *Sukhooma*
Headache *Suda' ras/waja' ras*
Pregnant *Haamel*
Prescription *Wasfa/rashetta*

Stomach ache *Waja' feel bat-n*
Sun-block cream *Marham wagee min ashat al shams*
Sanitary towels/tampons *Fuwat saHiyya leel Hareem*

LANGUAGE DIFFICULTIES

Do you speak English/French/German *Tatkallam ingleezi/fransawi/almaani?*
I understand (by a man) *Ana fahim*
I understand (by a woman) *Ana fahma*
I don't understand (by a man) *Ana ma fahim*
I don't understand (by a woman) *Ana ma fahma*
I don't speak Arabic *Ma atkallam arabi*
Could you write it down, please? *Mumkin tiktbha lee, min fadlak?*
Speak more slowly *Takalam shwai shwai*

SERVICES

The bank *Al bank*
Post office *Maktab al bareed*
Telephone *Al telefon/al hataf*

I want to change... *Ana abga asrif...*
Money *Floos*
Travellers' cheques *Sheikat seeyaHeeya*
Embassy *As safara*

SHOPPING

Where can I buy...?' *Wein agdar ashtiri...?*
Do you have...(to a man)? *Indik?*
Do you have... (to a woman)? *Indich?*
What is this? *Shoo Hadha?*
How much? *Bikam?*
How many? *Kam?*
It's too expensive *Ghalee/ghalia wa'id (m/f)*
There isn't (any) *Mafee (walashai)*
Can I look at it? *Mumkin ashoof il?*
What time does it open? *Sa'a kam yeftaH?*
What time does it close? *Sa'a kam yebannad?*

SIGHTSEEING

Where is the...? *Wein al...?*
Beach *Il shaat'i*
Souk *Al souq*
Mosque *Al masjid*
Museum *Al matHaf*
The Old City *Al madina al qadima*
Tourism office *Maktab al seeyaHa*

USEFUL PHRASES

Good/OK *Kweis/tayib/zein*
No problem *Mafee mushkala*
Impossible *Mish mumkin*
It doesn't matter/I don't mind *Ma'alish*
God willing (when talking about any future event or wish) *Insha'allah*
I like (Dubai) *Ana bHib (dubay)*
I don't like... *Ana ma bHib*
Excuse me (to a man) *Lau samaHt*
Excuse me (to a woman) *Lau samaHti*
After you *Atfaddal*

83

Museums and Galleries

Frankly, few come here for the culture. For most, Dubai and Abu Dhabi are all about beaches, bars and shopping, swish hotels and fancy restaurants. After all, luxury here is very affordable. But you don't have to dig deep to uncover the fascinating history of these two towns. Dubai and Abu Dhabi's museums are well worth visiting for the light they shed on the cities' past. Meanwhile, the burgeoning art scene in both cities is beginning to make the world wake up and take note.

BUR DUBAI
Dubai Museum
Al Fahidi Fort, off Al Fahidi Square, Bastakia; tel: 04-353 1862; www.dubaitourism.co.ae; Sat–Thur 8.30am–8.30pm, Fri 2.30–8.30pm; admission charge; map p.130 B2; Metro: Al Fahidi

Housed in the Al Fahidi fort, the interactive Dubai Museum covers all aspects of the city's history and development, combining genuine antiques and artefacts with video footage, photos, life-size dioramas and even a recreated creek-side souk. A visit is a great introduction to the city and will inform your trip around town – such as noticing the old tradition of decorating windows and doors which still continues in Bastakia.
SEE ALSO CHILDREN, P.39

Heritage & Diving Village
Off Al Khaleej Road, Al Shindaga; tel: 04-393 7151; www.dubaitourism.co.ae; Sun–Thur 8.30am–10pm, Fri–Sat 4–10pm; free; map p.130 A3

Above: explore the city's past at the Dubai Museum.

When open, the neighbouring 'villages' provide an all too rare and precious insight into traditional Emirati culture, including arts, crafts and even cooking. Craftsmen give live displays using methods passed down from generation to generation for centuries.
SEE ALSO CHILDREN, P.40

The Majlis Gallery
House No.19, Al Musalla Roundabout, Al Fahidi Street, Bastakia; tel: 04-353 6233; www.themajlisgallery.com; Sat–Thur 10am–6pm; free; map p.130 B2; Metro Al Fahidi

Set up in 1979, the Majlis Gallery prides itself on 'the pivotal part it played in bringing art and artists to the UAE'. Set in a lovingly restored courtyard house, the Majlis Gallery exhibits (and sells) all manner of art, from paintings and ceramics to furniture, glassware and sculptures. The gallery represents over 60 Middle Eastern and international artists and hosts changing exhibitions.

XVA Gallery
Building No.15a, Behind Majlis Gallery, Al Seef Road, Bastakia; tel: 04-353 5383; www.xvagallery.com; Sat–Thur 9am–7pm, Fri 10am–5pm; free; map p.130 B2; Metro: Al Fahidi

One of Dubai's foremost galleries, it's also one of its most attractive. Set in a restored courtyard house-cum-hotel with a

Left: sculpture along Sheikh Zayed Road.

2003, the gallery also provides advice on artists and the art market if you're looking for an investment.

Courtyard Gallery & Café
6A Street, Al Quoz 3, off Exit 43, Sheikh Zayed Road; tel: 04-347 9090; www.courtyardgallery dubai.com; Sun–Thur 10am–6pm; free

Part of an attractive cobbled courtyard complex that contains other galleries, craft and interior design shops, the Courtyard Gallery and Café is a lovely place to spend a morning. The Courtyard was the first gallery to host exhibitions by famous international artists; its emphasis is still global, with exhibitions ranging from 'Russian Chocolate Art' to 'Arte de España'. Since 2004, it has hosted

Abu Dhabi has its own annual art fair (www.abudhabiartfair.ae). Since 2011 it's been held at the UAE Pavilion. This pavilion was brought all the way from Shanghai, moved piece by piece. It's new home can now be found next to Manarat Al Saadiyat on Saadiyat Island.

If you're in Dubai mid-March, don't miss the annual art fair, **Art Dubai**. Launched in 2007, it was the UAE's first art fair. During the five–day festival, all the cities' galleries host special exhibitions, and in Bastakia, a kind of fringe festival, **Bastakia Art Fair**, runs for two weeks, organised by some of the city's independent galleries. You can expect the city to host nearly 100 galleries from all across the world.

DUBAI: SHEIKH ZAYED ROAD
Artspace
Level 2, Building No.3, DIFC Gate Village Building, DIFC; tel: 04-323 0820; www.artspace-dubai.com; Sat–Thur 10am–8pm; free; map p.12; Metro: Financial Centre

Hosting regularly changing and well-respected exhibitions of mainly paintings and sculpture, Artspace gallery is a popular spot among collectors of contemporary Middle Eastern and Iranian Art, whether amateur or professional, private or corporate. Founded in

bohemian café at its middle, it's a social and vibrant place. The gallery generally represents established Middle Eastern artists. Exhibitions, which change approximately every month, usually focus on fine art, but sometimes photography and sculpture too. There's usually even a resident artist or two staying in rented rooms. The XVA Gallery is also an organiser of the Bastikiya Art Fair each March.
SEE ALSO BARS AND CAFÉS, P.31; HOTELS, P.71

Right: Majlis Gallery.

The whole world knows about Dubai's meteoric rise from the desert; now word of a different development is slowly getting out: the city's exploding art scene. Until recently, art was considered a pastime in the UAE, not a profession, and schools rarely taught it. With more progressive educational institutes such as Dubai's Zayed University beginning to offer the subject, with the impact of Emiratis returning from art studies abroad, and the groundswell of interest sparked by local efforts such as Sharjah's Biennial in 2003, things began to change. In 2006, the British Museum sparked outside interest with its exhibition on contemporary Middle Eastern art. Christie's hit the headlines when it staged its first auction in Dubai. In 2007, Art Dubai and ArtParis Abu Dhabi, the UAE's first art festivals, were launched. In 2008, Bonhams staged its first auction. Phillips de Pury held its first in 2009. In the meantime, galleries, art courses and workshops are sprouting across Dubai, and investors are gathering. Abu Dhabi, meanwhile, is busy building its very own Louvre and Guggenheim.

a popular annual exhibition showcasing international women's art entitled 'Women in Art'.

Cuadro Fine Art Gallery
Building No.10, DIFC Gate Village, DIFC; tel: 04-425 0400; www.cuadroart.com; Sun–Thur 10am–8pm, Sat noon–6pm; free; map p.12; Metro: Financial Centre

According to its mission statement, Cuadro is 'committed to discovering, exhibiting and promoting innovative artists from the Middle East and around the world'. Exhibitions here are well chosen, well-lit and well displayed, and have an exciting range. Recent exhibitions range from photographs taken by Palestinian children of life in Lebanese refugee camps to an exhibition of monumental bronze sculptures of ants.

Flying House
25 Street, off 12A Street, two blocks behind Al Quoz Bowling Centre, Muscat Road, Al Quoz; tel: 04-265 3365; www.the-flyinghouse.com; free

If you're remotely interested in Emirati art, this is the place to come. The

Pick up if you can the new and excellent, tri-annual publication *Art Map*, available free from galleries and some bookshops, which covers all the current art exhibitions, events and festivals, as well as listing most galleries in Dubai and Abu Dhabi along with maps, contact details and often a short summary of the focus of the gallery. You can also check out: www.artinthecity.com. This website also gives details of ArtBuses which shuttle visitors around on a guided tour of the Emirates' main galleries, studios and art fairs.

excellent Flying House is a non-profit-making institution that seeks both to document the major contemporary artists and to nurture the new ones. Its fine collection spans the whole life of the UAE as a nation and includes all the 'greats' including Hassan Sharif, generally considered the 'father' of Emirati art, as well as Hussain Sharif and Fatma Loofah, and 'second generations' such as Mohammed Ahmed Ibrahim. It's open by appointment only, so call ahead.

Gallery Isabelle van den Eynde

Street 8 Al Serkal Avenue, Unit 17, Al Quoz 1; tel: 04-323 5052; ivde.net; Sat–Thur 10am–7pm; free

Priding itself on a quest to find new artistic talent, Gallery Isabelle van den Eynde's exhibitions sometimes show a little more daring and adventure than some of its fellow-galleries. Its main focus is on Middle Eastern and Gulf artists and its aim is to nurture future talent. Converted from an old warehouse, it boasts plenty of space, and the changing exhibitions include fine art, photography and sculpture. It's a must-stop for Dubai's art intelligentsia.

Green Art Gallery

Al Quoz 1, Street 8, Alserhal Avenue, Unit 28; tel: 04-346 9305; www.gagallery.com; Sat–Thur 10am–7pm; free
Established in 1995, Green Art is one of Dubai's oldest galleries, and was the first to give a proper platform to Middle Eastern artists. Originally it was located in Jumeira but it has moved to dusty Al Quoz; its warehouses lend themselves very well to the open modern spaces ideal for displaying art. The gallery also prides itself on its contribution to the development of Dubai's art scene, as well as its part in launching the career of now-established Arab artists. Exhibitions currently focus on both established and up-and-coming artists from the Middle East as well as from North Africa, and are

popular and well respected among local art aficionados.

thejamjar

Behind Dubai Garden Centre, between Habitat and Chevrolet Insportz, off Exit 39, Sheikh Zayed Road, Al Quoz; tel: 04-341 7303; www.thejamjar dubai.com; Mon–Thur, Sat 10am–8pm, Fri 2–8pm; free
Probably the most proactive gallery in Dubai, thejamjar involves itself in all sorts of community activities, as well as numbering among the city's best galleries. Though focusing mainly on Asian art from a diverse range of countries including India and Pakistan, Japan, Korea, China and Hong Kong, the gallery also provides a platform for regional artists, including Emirati art students. The gallery also offers the DIY Painting Studio, open to all, including families, where you can

> Dubai's exciting and burgeoning art scene is emerging in three main places: the Al Quoz industrial area east of Jumeira and Sheikh Zayed Road; the new Dubai International Financial Centre (DIFC) at the heart of Sheikh Zayed Road; and in Bastakia, the old historical quarter in Bur Dubai. Additionally, a couple of galleries have sprouted like blown seeds in Jumeira. Exciting newcomers to the scene in addition to those listed here include: Basement, Art Sawa, the Ayyam Gallery (all in Al Quoz), the Opera in the DIFC and Tashkeel Gallery in Nad al Sheba. Be sure to bring this book (and its maps) with you. The galleries are notoriously difficult to locate in all areas and are not listed on the city's maps.

come to create that long-imagined masterpiece. All equipment (including an artist's apron) is provided, and there's a choice of canvas. Art discussions are also hosted here as well as an excellent range of artist-led workshops designed for children, families and adults that range from lomography to recycled art and creating murals.

Meem Gallery

Umm Suqueim Road, off Interchange 4, Al Quoz; tel: 04-347 7883; www.meem.ae; Sat–Thur 10am–7pm; free
The modest aim of the Meem is to 'present the greatest contemporary Arabic art by the greatest contemporary Arab artists'. Well managed, well funded and well connected (to international galleries and art collectors), it does. The Meem is a great place to come for the low-down on the current Arab art scene, as well as to see some leading international artists. A purchase here is also likely to be a good investment, though prices aren't cheap.

Meydan Museum

Meydan Racecourse, Al Meydan Road; Nad Al Sheba; tel: 04-327 0000; www.meydan.ae; map p.12
The spectacular racecourse contains a new museum of equine heritage with displays of the history and heritage of horseracing.
SEE ALSO RACING, P.98

Third Line

Between Courtyard gallery and Spinney's Warehouse, behind Times Square, 6 Street, off Exit

Above: work by Shezad Dawood at the Third Line, *p.87.*

43, Sheikh Zayed Road, Al Quoz; tel: 04-341 1367; www.thethirdline.com; Sat–Thur 11am–8pm; free
Considered one of Dubai's most avant-garde galleries, exhibitions focus on contemporary Middle Eastern art. Many of the artists represented show more innovative and genre-breaking styles than those found in galleries elsewhere. Even if you don't like the art, you can be sure that a visit here will make you pause for thought.

Total Arts Gallery
Inside the Courtyard complex, 6 Street, Al Quoz 3, off Exit 43, Sheikh Zayed Road; tel: 04-347 5050; www.courtyard-uae.com; Sat–Thur 10am–7pm; free
One of the oldest galleries in Dubai and the first to open in the Al Quoz area, the trailblazing Total represents mainly Middle Eastern artists, some established, some not. Exhibitions change every four to six weeks, and this well-run gallery also hosts regular art events.

XVA Gallery DIFC
Building 7, DIFC Gate Village, DIFC; 04-358 5117; www.xva-gallery.com; Sun–Thur

10am–6pm; map p.12 ; Metro: Financial Centre
This is the lastest addition to the XVA brand. In this location the well-established XVA reinvents itself in an entirely contemporary way (the original gallery is still in Bastakia).

ABU DHABI: CORNICHE
Emirates Palace
West Corniche, tel: 02-690 9000; www.swissartgateuae.com; 10am–10pm; free; map p.136 A3
Though much better known as Abu Dhabi's

A new kid on the Dubai art block is the excellent **Souk Al Bastakia** (tel: 04-321 7114; www.souqalbastakiya.com; free; map p.130 B2), an art focused street market that takes place every Saturday from 10am to sunset during the winter. As well as featuring over 50 stalls selling everything from arts, crafts and book to jewellery, fashion and accessories, there are live musical performances, a dedicated kids corner, and the **Souq Café** (Fri, Sat 11am–10pm). A live painting studio is also run in conjunction with thejamjar art gallery, and workshops open to all are put on.

famous palatial hotel, the Emirates Palace is also one of the city's leading art spaces, with regularly changing art exhibitions and events. From mid-January to mid-April 2009, the Palace held the very first – and ground breaking – comprehensive exhibition of Emirati artists. The website gives details of the art being shown at Emirates Palace as well as venues like Yas Viceroy in Abu Dhabi. Currently, there is also a permanent exhibition detailing the hugely ambitious and exciting designs for Saadiyat island which include plans and models to expand the art and culture scene including the Zayad National Museum, a new Guggenheim, Louvre, a Performing Arts Centre and a Maritime Museum.

Heritage Village
Near Marina Mall, Breakwater; tel: 02-681 4455; Mon–Thur 9am–1pm, 5–9pm, Fri 5–9pm, Sat 9am–1pm, 5–9pm; free; map p.136 B4
If you're not planning to travel outside the city to more rural areas, this open museum gives a good idea of pre-oil, pre-industri-

alised Abu Dhabi. There are workshops where craftsmen demonstrate their traditional skills such as metal work and pottery.

CENTRAL AND SOUTH ABU DHABI
Eclectic
Mashreq Bank/Patchi Building, Khalidiyah Street No. 7; tel: 02-666 5158; email: eclectic@eim.ae; Sat–Thur 10.30am–1.30pm, 5–9pm; free
Eclectic is well named: the gallery exhibits a diverse collection of both period and modern Eastern artefacts that range from Arabic furniture, sculpture and silver, to kilims, ceramic, textiles and designer jewellery, originating from regions as wide-ranging as China, the Levant and North Africa. The gallery also exhibits artwork by established contemporary Middle Eastern artists.

National Library
Opposite Central Bus Station, intersection of Delma Street and Murour Road; tel: 02-657 6034; www.library.adach.ae; Sun–Thur 8am–10pm, Sat 10am–8pm; free; map p.137 D1
In the National Library,

there is a collection of over 4,000 ancient Arab and Islamic manuscripts covering a variety of topics including literature, religion and science.

Qibab Gallery
Opposite Abu Dhabi Coop, Villa 3, Street 15, Al Bateen; tel: 02-665 2360; www.qihabgallery.com; Sat–Thur 10am–1pm, 5–9pm; free; map p.136 B2
Though specialising particularly in Iraqi art, the Qibab has an excellent programme of changing exhibitions (usually every three weeks) by modern artists from countries as diverse as Malaysia, Iran and Egypt, as well as Gulf

countries. 'Dedicated to the promotion of national and international contemporary art', Qibab also claims to have its finger on the pulse of the regional art scene. Exhibitions range from fine art and calligraphy to sculpture and photography.

Salwa Zeidan
2nd Floor, Villa 256, Al Khaleej Al Arabi Street No.30; tel: 02-666 9656; www.salwazeidangallery.com; Sun–Thur 10am–7pm, Fri–Sat by appointment; free; map p.136 C2
Run by gallery namesake Salwa Zeidan, herself an artist from Lebanon, the centro's aim is to represent established, contemporary Middle Eastern and international artists in most media. Exhibitions are eclectic and well chosen and range from fine art, sculpture and photography to installation and even performance art. This gallery has plans to relocate and then will only offer private viewings.

Above: Abu Dhabi Heritage Village.
Left: appreciating fine art in Abu Dhabi.

89

Nightlife

Dubai, hotly pursued by Abu Dhabi, boasts the best nightlife in the Gulf. Increasingly attracting big-name bands and DJs, the cities also have talented residents to call upon. Their repertoire is wide-ranging: from Arabic and Latino to hip-hop, funk and African, though house and R&B are currently most heard. Nightspots also vary widely: from Dubai beach bar to über-hip lounge bar, OTT dance club, old-worldly expat pub, or the more gritty immigrant joints in the backstreets. Thursday and Fridays (Dubai's weekend) are the big nights, though DJs play every night (except during Ramadan).

DUBAI: DEIRA
Alpha
Le Méridien hotel, Airport Road; tel: 04-702 2560; www.lemeridiendubai.com; daily noon–3am, restaurant and lounge 6pm–3am, live entertainment Sat–Thur 9:30pm onwards, Fri 10:30pm onwards; map p.135 D3
This venue tries to cater to everyone with its relaxing garden terrace, four sophisticated bars, two restaurants, and a sushi bar. Mostly people come for cocktails and the unpretentious dancefloor. It's particularly popular on a Friday after brunch.

BUR DUBAI
Chi@TheLodge
Al Nasr Leisureland, just off Al Garhoud Bridge; tel: 04-337 9470; www.lodgedubai.com; daily 9pm–3am; map p.133 E2
Since refurbishment, Chi has become a firm feature on the Dubai club scene. Its diehard devotees love the gigantic garden-terrace, the über-cool all-white hip hop room (with occasional funk and soul), and the plush VIP room. It may lack innovation, but with a vibe, music and ambience to suit most tastes, it's certainly a crowd-pleaser. Its Thursday and Friday nights are famous.

People by Crystal
Raffles Dubai, Wafi, off Sheikh Rashid Road; tel: 050–297 2097; daily 10pm–3am, map p.A1; Metro: Healthcare City
2012 Winner of the Best Club in *Time Out*'s Nightlife Awards, People by Crystal is flashy and ultra-glamourous and gets

Left and below: stylish clubs dominate the scene.

Comedy

As well as visiting bands and DJs, Dubai and Abu Dhabi see a reasonable share of international comedy acts, which are particularly popular with Western expats. Venues alternate but usually take place in hotels and clubs from between 8pm and 9.30pm. For current acts, check out the website of the **Laughter Factory** (www.the laugherfactory.com), which has connections with London and Manchester's Comedy Stores.

very busy. It is well worth making a reservation if you want to join the party. It's located in the tip of the Raffles pyramid and has wonderful views of the city if you can take your eyes off the dazzling decadence of the club's interior.

Rock Bottom Café

Regent Palace Hotel, Al Waleed Road; tel: 04-396 3888; www.rameehotels.com; daily noon–3am

Left: the 360° club.

Jekyll and Hyde-like, the Rock Bottom Café transforms from family-friendly 70s steakhouse during the day, to late-night joint where you head when everything else has closed. Well named it may be, but its combination of house bands and resident DJ, plus the infamous club cocktail, the Bullfrog, pulls in the punters without fail. It's a bit dingy and down-market, but all great fun.

Submarine

Dhow Palace Hotel, Kuwait Street; tel: 04-359 9992; www.dhowpalacehotel.com; daily 6pm–3am; map p.132 C3
In keeping with the marine theme of its location inside the Dhow Palace, this new club's interior is startlingly submarine-like, complete with tube-like interior, portholes and neon lighting. The club boasts a resident band, decent DJs, state of the art lasers and even some smoke machines for added atmosphere.

DUBAI: JUMEIRA
360°

Jumeirah Beach Hotel, Jumeira Road; tel 04-406 8999; www.jumeirah.com; Sun–Wed 5pm–2am, Thur and Sat club 5pm–2am, lounge 5pm–2am, Fri club 4pm–2am, lounge 4pm–3am; map p.10
Relaunched and made even more glitzy in 2012, this staple of the Dubai club scene pleased its punters and won an award for 'best club' of 2013. Set in the sea on its own pier, with grandstand views of the Burj Al Arab, and attracting all of Dubai's 'beautiful people', 360° is as glam as you can get and is the archetypal be-seen Dubai club. On weekdays, the vibe is laid-back and mellow, attracting *shisha*-smoking, sofa-slouching punters. On Friday, it's ramped-up electronica. Drinks are not cheap and it can be difficult to get into at the weekend. On Friday and Saturday guests have to register online for entry before 8pm.

91

Alcohol

A night on the town in Dubai or Abu Dhabi can be costly. With club entry fees, drinks, tips and taxis, you can easily spend Dh1,000. Entry to most bars and pubs is free, but entry to clubs (depending on the night and the act) can cost anything between Dh50–350. Depending on the locale, a pint of beer can cost between Dh25–45, a glass of wine Dh25 to Dh150. Many hotels tack on a 10 percent service charge to boot.

Boudoir

Dubai Marine Beach Resort & Spa, Jumeira Road; tel: 04-346 1111; www.dxbmarine.com/ Boudoir; daily 7.30pm–3am
Arguably Dubai's most exclusive club, Boudoir is appropriately well-named with its scarlet swags, crystal chandeliers, gilded-framed mirrors and oil paintings. The decadent decor creates a decadent vibe and attracts a predominantly Franco-Lebanese crowd glammed up to the nines, along with the city's celebs and shakers. The music typically spans lounge, house, funk, hip-hop, pop and rock.

Sho Cho

Dubai Marine Beach Resort & Spa, Jumeira Road; tel: 04-346 1111; www.dbxmarine.com/ Sho-Cho; daily 7pm–3am
The place to be seen among Dubai's indefatigable fashionistas is the achingly super-hip Sho Cho. Japanese goes nautical in the style of its decor, seafood menu and minimalism (right down to the ingenious neon-lit fish tanks, sushi finger food and Manga movies projected on the walls), it also brags a terrace with stunning ocean views. On most nights you'll need to phone ahead to secure a reservation.

Taxis

One advantage of the bars' and clubs' location inside hotels is that taxis are usually easy to come by or call (though at weekends, you'll have to join the queue). Both public and private taxis serve hotels. The former are metered (with a starting fare of Dh10 day and night), and are reasonably priced and generally reliable and honest. The latter, which serve the major hotels and shopping malls, are also metered but charge at least 30 percent more. Note that traffic jams can be a major problem on Thursdays and Fridays. If possible, avoid journeying across districts; you'll spend most of the evening in the back of a cab. If you can neither find a cab nor hail one, then try calling one of the numbers below. They usually come within 10 to 15 minutes, though you can wait much longer at peak times.
Dubai Transport Company: tel: 04-208 0808
Metro Taxis: tel: 04-267 3222

Trilogy

Souk Madinat Jumeirah, Jumeira Road; tel: 04-366 6917; www.jumeirah.com, daily 10pm–3am; map p.14
Three floors of pumping music and cocktails make for a lively venue. Attracts some of the biggest electronic music acts around.

DUBAI: SHEIKH ZAYED ROAD
Cavalli Club

Fairmont Dubai hotel, Sheikh Zayed Road; tel: 04-332 9260; www.fairmontdubai.com; daily 8pm–3am, map p.132 B1; Metro: World Trade Centre
Fashion designer Roberto

Left: dress to impress if you want to get through the door.

Door Policy

Some clubs – and bars – have notoriously rigid door policies. It pays to come – and dress – prepared. For entrance to the more glam, hip and trendy venues, the following items constitute fashion faux-pas (and actually constitute a 'banned item' at the door):

• Sport strips of any type
• Ripped clothing, even jeans
• Hot pants for girls
• Swimwear
• Baseball caps
• Sandals
• Trainers
• Bandanas

Under 21 years won't get through the door, and, boys beware, many clubs operate an anti-single-male policy (or even anti-bachelor groups). If you want to guarantee getting in, hook up with a girl.

Above: contemporary club culture sits uneasily beside traditional Arab values.

Cavalli has lent his name and his brash sense of style to this restaurant and club. It's decked out lavishly in animal prints and shimmering crystals. The menu is Italian with some international flavours. Dress up for this club; it's all about fashion, luxury and drinking a cocktail in the spotlight.

Zinc

Mezzanine Floor, Crowne Plaza Hotel, Sheikh Zayed Road, tel: 04-331 1111; www.szrdining. com, open 10pm–3am

Recently revamped but still refreshingly free of pretension and posing, and hosting a steady stream of visiting bands and DJs, is the ever-popular Zinc. It's not the hippest or the smartest, but with its changing nights (including salsa and comedy), 'special promotions' (on food and drink), and wide range of music from R&B to tech house and reggae, it's worth checking out.

Zuma Bar & Lounge

Gate Village 06, DIFC, tel: 04-425 5660, www.zumarestaurant.com, Sat–Wed noon–2am, Thur–Fri noon–2am; map p.12; Metro: Financial Centre
This funky Japanese restaurant comes highly recommended but it's also an alluring place for some sociable drinks. The sake bar and lounge buzz in the evening as professionals chat and relax after a hard day's work. Super trendy and modern Zuma reflects Dubai's ability to lay on a lounge bar fit for any of the coolest cities in the world.

Left: Trilogy.   93

ABU DHABI: CORNICHE
Cinnabar
Hilton International Abu Dhabi, Corniche Road West; tel: 02-681 1900; Sat–Mon 10pm–2am; Tue–Fri 10pm–3.30am; map p.136 B3

Home of the former Tequilana, the revamped, relaunched venue includes arguably the best sound system in the city, in a club that's already proving one of the places to be. Chic and classy, Cinnabar hosts both international and resident DJs as well as live bands. On Tuesdays between 10pm and midnight there's free sparkling wine for women.

Etoiles
Emirates Palace Hotel, Corniche West; tel: 02-690 8960; www.etoilesuae.com; club Mon–Fri 11pm–3am, restaurant Sun–Fri 7pm–11:30pm; map p.136 A3

Typical Night Out
For a Dubai or Abu Dhabi hard party-goer, a typical weekend evening might go something like this: a post-work drink with colleagues in the city, or a cocktail with friends at a beach bar following a swim, whilst watching the sun go down over the sea; then dinner in a nearby restaurant on a terrace with a view; a drink in a lounge bar with more friends; a trip to a club, then a falafel or *shawarma* pit-stop, followed by hitting a final club or lounge bar. If you're planning to hit the clubs, go late (around 1am) when the locals do; or to beat the queues at both the door and the bar, come a bit earlier. And come with lots of cash or plenty of credit: entrance fees range from Dh50 to Dh350 or more, depending on the band or DJ.

Recently revamped, Etoiles has rapidly turned into one of the city's faves. Glam and glitzy, befitting its home in the Emirates Palace, it attracts the well healed and occasional celeb. It's so busy at weekends that you'll need to make a reservation, unless you come early. Tuesday 9pm–3am is ladies' night which includes free entry and free champagne cocktails.

Zenith
Sheraton Abu Dhabi Resort & Towers, off As–Salaam St; tel: 02-697 0224; www.zenithabudhabi.com; Tue–Sat 9pm–3.30am; map p.137 D3

With a circular dance floor set over two floors (the upper section a gallery), the spaceship-like Zenith attracts a well-heeled, self-conscious and dressed-up crowd, particularly at weekends.

CENTRAL AND SOUTH ABU DHABI
Left Bank
Souk Qaryat Al Beri, next to Shangri-La hotel, Bain Al Jesran; tel: 02-558 1680;

Right: ladies' nights help to even out the crowd in male-dominated Dubai.

Sun–Wed 5pm–2am, Thur–Sat noon–3am

A fresh addition to the scene but already a firm fixture with the Abu Dhabi It crowd, the Left Bank is a bar-cum-restaurant boasting a cool retro interior, stunning views from the balcony across the water to the new Grand Mosque and decent cocktails. DJs play a mixture of house, techno and trip hop, and sometimes there are live bands playing jazz, blues or rock.

Level Lounge
Crowne Plaza Hotel, Hamdan Mohamed Street; tel: 02-616 6101; www.cpauhoutlets.com; daily 5pm–2am; map p.137 D3

With DJs from Dubai playing good house and techno music, its outdoor location, relaxed atmosphere and famous 'pool party' on Friday, the Level attracts trendy clubbers by the lounge-load, particularly at weekends, when you'll need to book.

Because hotels and sporting venues are the only places permitted to serve alcohol, they can feel a bit like social ghettos. Very few local Emiratis frequent these places (drinking alcohol is *haram* – forbidden – according to the Quran, and by law, alcohol can only be served to non-Muslims), and many are further segregated consciously or unconsciously by other social parameters, whether national, class-related or fashion-focused. This can be an advantage – where else can you dance in a super-glamorous, Beiruti-style club, drink Guinness in a spit-and-sawdust Irish-themed pub, or take the limelight in a karaoke bar that could have come straight out of Manila? Butterflying from ghetto to ghetto is half of Dubai and Abu Dhabi's fun, but if straying onto other's territory, it pays to dress (and act) accordingly, or you may not be made to feel very welcome. Sadly, a few places in Dubai have even been accused of operating overtly racist door policies.

Sax Restaurant Club

Le Royal Meridien, Khalifa Bin Zayed Street, Al Markaziyah; tel: 02-674 2020; www.leroyalmeridien abudhabi.com; Sat–Wed 7pm–2.30am; Thur, Fri 7pm–3.30am; map p.137 D3
Something of an Abu Dhabi institution and still the most popular late-night bar in town, Sax is Manhattan-chic in style, and has a reputation for good in-house DJs, decent live music, well-conceived cocktails and great food.

Sho Cho

Souk Qaryat Al Beri, next to Shangri-La Hotel, Bain Al Jesran; tel: 02-558 1117; Sun–Thur noon–3pm, 6pm–midnight; Fri–Sat noon–3am
Like its sophisticated cousin in Dubai, this hipper than hip new Japanese-themed club is all about neon-lit minimalism, cool, stylish interiors, fine sushi and fluorescent cocktails. There's both indoor and outdoor seating, great views and in-house DJs playing mixed music from chilled-out tunes to 80s beats on Fridays.

YAS ISLAND
Allure by Cipriani

Yas Island Yacht Club, Yas Island; tel: 02-673 8301; www.nightcluballure.com
With stunning views, particularly at sunset, Allure has much to offer. A resident DJ plays the latest R & B hits in an ultra-glamorous atmosphere. This is the place to spot celebs and has the seal of approval from *Ahlan!* (the Middle East's equivalent of *Hello!* magazine).

Left: Abu Dhabi's Corniche at night.

Pampering

For many visitors it's what you 'do' in Dubai, along with the fine-dining and shopping. Pampering's also part of the 'Jumeira-Jane' (expat) lifestyle. No surprise, then, that all the cities' better hotels boast a 'spa' offering any number of treatments. Even if you're not really a 'pamper panda', this might be the time to try it – the boys as well as the girls; the men in these parts (Emiratis and expats) are much less coy about personal grooming. The top places are not cheap, though considering the assiduous service and sometimes spectacular settings, it represents real value for money.

SPAS & BEAUTY TREATMENTS

DUBAI

1847
Boulevard Mall, Emirates Towers, Sheikh Zayed Road; tel: 04-330 1847; daily 9am–10pm; map p.12; Metro: Emirates Towers
This high-class 'grooming salon' for men offers everything from massages, manicures and facials to haircuts and pedicures. Branches are also in Grosvenor House Hotel, Jumeirah Beach Residence and Mirdif City Centre.

Amara
Park Hyatt Dubai, Next to Dubai Creek Golf and Yacht Club, Al Garhoud Road; tel: 04-602 1234; www.dubai.park.hyatt .com; daily 9am–10pm; map p.134 C3
At arguably Dubai's most exclusive spa, Amara's cosseted customers enjoy a private courtyard-garden, a complimentary foot bath, post-treatment refreshments and day-long access to the pool and gym.

Assawan Spa & Health Club
18th Floor, Burj Al Arab hotel, Jumeira Road; tel: 04-301 7338; www.burj-al-arab; daily 6.30am–10.30pm; map p.14
For luxurious treatments in the most lavish of Arabic surroundings, the Assawan is unbeatable, though so are its prices. Treatments range from organic caviar-derived wraps to La Prairie facials and Chakra balancing hot stone therapy.

Left: spas push the cities' reputation for luxury to the limit.

Cleopatra's Spa
Wafi Shopping Mall; Sheikh Rashid Road; tel: 04-324 7700; www.cleopatrasspaandwell ness.com; female spa daily 9am–9pm; male spa Sun–Wed 10am–10pm, Thur–Sat 10am–9pm; map p.134 A1; Metro: Healthcare City
Known for its opulent surroundings and attentive service, Cleopatra also offers more unusual treatments including 'exotic facials', body sculpting and massages combining aromatherapy with hot stone treatment.

Health and Beauty Institute
One&Only Royal Mirage hotel, Al Sufouh Road; tel: 04-399 9999; www.royalmirage.oneandonly resorts.com; daily 9am–9pm; Oriental Hammam 04-315 2130 daily 8:30am–10pm; ladies only 8:30am–2pm gentlemen only 8pm–10pm; map p.14
Spreading 2,000 sq m (21,500 sq ft) over two floors, the Health and

Left: couples can enjoy simultaneous treatments.

Booking a spa treatment sometimes entitles you to complementary access to the hotel's facilities including pools and beaches. If you want the latter without the former, some hotels sell day passes that grant access to all facilities.

8:30am–11am; map p.137 E3
Eden offers everything from hammams and 'aquamedic pools' to its own beach. Treatments include mineral baths, aromatherapy and Ayurveda therapy.

Beauty Centre offers exceptional facilities including Jacuzzis, steam rooms, whirlpool and a wonderful traditional hamman, as well as its own fragrant products.

H2O Male Spa

Emirates Towers; tel: 04–319 8181; www.jumeirahemirates towers.com; daily 9am–11pm; map p.12; Metro: Emirates Towers
The avant-garde H2O offers man-treatments that range from waxing and facials to sessions in the stress-busting Flotation Pool or the sure-fire, post-partying remedying Oxygen Lounge.

Mandara Spa

The H Hotel, Sheikh Zayed Road, Trade Centre Roundabout; tel: 04-501 8888; www.h-hotel.com; daily 9am–10pm; map p.132 B1
Combining the latest techniques with age-old oriental methods, Mandara offers a kind of spa-fusion experience. The 'four-hand massage' is a big hit among stressed city execs.

Talise

Al Qasr, Madinat Jumeira, Jumeira Road; tel: 04-366 6818; www.madinatjumeirah. com/spa; daily 9am–10pm; map p 14
Ranked among the city's top spas, the Talise is hard to beat for its setting amid landscaped gardens, or for its state-of-the-art treatments and massages. It's not the cheapest, but it's certainly worth a one-off splurge.

Willow Stream Spa

Fairmont Dubai, Sheikh Zayed Road; tel 04-311 8800; www.fairmont.com; daily 9am–10pm; map p.132 B1
Covering almost 4,000 sq m (40,000 sq ft), the faux Graeco-Roman Willow is the city's largest spa and offers its greatest range of treatments.

ABU DHABI

Eden Spa & Health Club

Le Méridien, 10th Street; tel: 02-697 4354; www.lemeridien abudhabi.com; daily 9am–11pm; ladies only Sat–Sun and Tue

Hiltonia Spa

Hilton International, Corniche Road West; tel: 02-632 7777; www.hilton.com; daily 8am–9pm; map p.136 B3
Clients here enjoy a wide choice of treatments – from thalassotherapy and reflexology to Indian head massage – plus full access to the hotel's facilities.

COSMETICS SHOPS

Cosmetics are sold in all the department stores but look out for Paris Gallery (www.parisgallery.com) which is the Middle East's top retailer of luxury goods, they offers a huge variety of skincare and fragrances.

Many of the malls have their own treatment rooms and nail bars. There's noticeably fewer of the plush surroundings of the hotel spas but it's certainly a convenient way to relax and have some pampering in between retail therapy. Lilypond has branches at Jumeirah's Town Centre mall, Mirdif City Centre and at JBR Rimal and JBR Amwaj in Dubai Marina.

Racing

T he Emiratis love their racing. Hosting the world's richest horse race, one of its most successful stables, and a stunning racecourse that out-dazzles the world's best, Dubai is positioning itself as the top spot in the world for horse racing. Both Dubai and Abu Dhabi dominate the region in another type of racing too: camel racing. Representing the most visible vestige of their Bedouin past, the ancient sport is a key part of traditional culture. A trip to the races is a must. With free entrance and a chance to get a precious peek into local culture, it's likely to form one of your most enjoyable and enduring memories.

HORSE RACING
Season and Times
The race season runs officially from November to March (sometimes also in October), and meetings are held in the afternoons or evenings. Usually six races run every half-hour from around 6pm to around 9pm. You can check for upcoming meets on the Emirates Racing Association website: www.emiratesracing.com

Racecourses
There are three main race-tracks in the UAE: the new Meydan City course in Dubai, the Abu Dhabi Equestrian Club and the less high-profile Jebel Ali in Dubai. There is also one in Sharjah.

Access and Dress Code
Open to all, access to the public enclosures is free, but to the clubhouse there's a charge. Children (supervised) are permitted into the public enclosures. Dress code is casual, except in the stands and clubhouse where 'smart-casual' (jacket and trousers) is stipulated. During the famous Dubai World Cup, race-goers come dressed to the nines, rather like Britain's Royal Ascot.

Spectators and participants at the legendary Dubai World Cup in March 2010, had the pleasure of experiencing the famous Nad Al Sheba racecourse and discovering that it had undergone not a facelift but a major transformation. Renamed **Meydan City** (*meydan* means public square or meeting place in Arabic), the multibillion-dollar complex will comprise top business, residential, sport and 'lifestyle' facilities, including a five-star hotel, five restaurants, and an IMAX cinema. Sport facilities will include the new **Dubai Racing Club** (www.dubairacing club.com), the delta-winged, futuristic grandstand with a capacity of 60,000 (one of the largest in the world), as well as state-of-the-art training and breeding facilities.

Betting and Prizes
Though gambling is not permitted by the Emirates (in accordance with Islamic principles), open competitions (such as the 'Pick 6' race cards) are held with cash and other prizes including cars for punters lucky enough to pick the first three finishers. For the race winners, cash prizes amount to a hefty US$20 million during the Dubai World Cup, making it the richest horse-racing cup in the world.

Jockeys
Races attract top jockeys, trainers and their horses from three continents: Europe (including Ireland), the US and Australia. If you come to a major race such as the Dubai World Cup, look out for famous Italian-born jockey Frankie Dettori.

Facilities
Food and beverages (including alcohol in the stands) are available, and there are toilets and free parking. For further details,

Left: camel racing at Al Marmoum.

as during the major public holidays. Check in advance as days and times change. Races start early in the morning, usually by 7 to 7.30am, and only last an hour or so. If you come in the off-season (and during the season), you can catch the camels training from 7am to 10am.

Camel Festival
The Dubai Camel Festival, which culminates in the Grand Final, usually takes place in the first 12 days of March.

Information
Race meetings are announced in local newspapers and TV. You can also telephone the tracks directly.

see the Dubai Racing Club website: www.dubairacing club.com

DUBAI

Dubai Racing Club
Meydan City Racecourse, off Al Ain Road, Nad Al Sheba; tel: 04-327 0000; Oct–Apr; www.meydan.ae; map p.12
There are normally, between six to seven races run during the evening. Races are also keenly attended by the Emirati royalty. Look out for Sheikh Mohammed, his family and entourage. The driving force behind the highly successful **Godolphin Stables**, he loves to watch his horses triumph.

ABU DHABI

Abu Dhabi Equestrian Club
Off 19th Street, Al Mushriff; tel: 02-445 5500; www.adec-web.com; Sun, Nov–Mar
Races usually run every half-hour from around 6pm.

Right: Animal Kingdom winning the $10 million Dubai World Cup.

CAMEL RACING
In former times, camel racing was only put on for special occasions such as during festivals or large society weddings. Today, it's both a national sport and an obsession.

Season and Times
The race season runs from October to March and meetings are held usually twice daily four times a week in Dubai (Saturday to Tuesday), and twice a week (Thursday and Friday) once daily in Abu Dhabi, as well

---

Camel Racing
Oct–Mar; Al Lisailli, Dubai
Unmissable for its colour, chaos and atmosphere.
Horse Racing
Nov–Apr; Meydan Racecourse; www.emiratesracing.com.
Owners of some world-class runners, the Emiratis love the races, a trip here is a must.

Based in both Dubai and Newmarket, England, the Al Maktoum-owned **Godolphin Racing** (www.Godolphin.com) is one of the most successful racing enterprises of all time. Named after one of the three original bloodstock stallions of modern thoroughbreds, the company has registered countless Group/Grade One wins in around a dozen countries. Wintering in Dubai, horses spend the summer in the UK. The stable's most famous product was racing prodigy Dubai Millennium, which won the 2000 Dubai World Cup by a staggering six lengths.

Races

The shortest race, just 3km (2 miles), is usually reserved for the younger, greener camels; the longest is 8km (5 miles). Races – short but furious – last six to seven minutes. The races attract camels and their cronies from all across the Gulf (bar Yemen). Normally around 120 camels compete in a day; for the grand final (usually in mid-March), up to 12,000 camels congregate from far and wide. After the races, it's down to business: much buying and selling among owners, trainers and breeders take place (including of baby camels); it's well worth hanging around for. If you're really lucky, you may get to sample *hashi* (roasted baby camel). Traditional dancing is sometimes put on before and particularly after races.

Racetracks

Most of the UAE's emirates boast camel racetracks, including Dubai and Abu Dhabi. The one lying outside Digdagga in Ras Al Khaimah is particularly well known, and well worth a visit if you're travelling in the area when races are running.

Jockeys

Since 2005, and in response to international pressure from human rights groups, the UAE has ceased the use of child jockeys. Instead, little remote-controlled robots resembling monkeys sit on top of their steeds, complete with racing silks and little whips.

Camels

Camels can reach speeds of up to 60kph (35mph) and are in their prime just after weaning, at the age of about one year. Both male and female camels compete in the racing; in fact female camels, lighter and slimmer, are often swifter at this age. Listen out for the names which can range from 'Colonel Kaddafi' and 'Gulf Air' to 'Carrefour '(the name of

Left and right: unlike horse racing, camel racing is drenched in the trappings of Bedouin culture.

Left: Sheikh Mohammed Al Maktoum with the Dubai World Cup.

the popular French low-cost hypermarket chain).

Access and Codes of Conduct

Races are open to all and free to all and dress code is definitely casual, but as the event attracts mainly Emirati men, women should dress conservatively. Beware, it can get very dusty. Photography is allowed.

Betting and Prizes

As with horse racing, gambling is not permitted but cash prizes are awarded to punters who can guess the finishers, but be sure to place your 'bets' before the start of the first race. Past prizes in Dubai have ranged from wads of cash to top-of-the-range Mercedes 4WDs and a ceremonial gold sword worth Dh150,000. The camel owners can win up to Dh50,000 for a single race.

Facilities

Food and beverages are available, as are toilets and free parking. The races also attract a good number of vendors and stalls, selling everything from camel blankets, hobbles and halters to vitamins, buckets and food supplements. They're well worth a wander.

DUBAI

Dubai Camel Racing Club

Al Lisailli, off Exit 37, Al Ain Road; tel: 04-832 6526; www.dubaicalendar.ae; usually mid-Oct–mid-Mar Sat–Tue 7–8.30am

In 2006, Dubai's principal camel-racing club moved from Nad Al Sheba to its new home in Al Lisailli on the Al Ain Road. Races take place twice a day, there's a morning session from 7 to 10am and and an afternoon session from 2 to 5pm. If you come here by taxi, you'll have to ask the driver to wait (on a meter), or you may get stranded. From Exit 37, take the first road to the right just before the small mosque and follow it to the stadium. Follow the road round the stadium to the group of buildings directly behind it. The Club lies around 40km (25 miles) from Dubai centre

(45 to 60 minutes by car).

The Dubai Camel Racing Club hosts the Dubai Camel Racing Festival which runs for 12 days in February with daily races. It features highly-trained camels from all over the Middle East of different ages and breeds. Call ahead for detailed information (tel: 055-676 0006).

ABU DHABI

Al Wathba Camel Racetrack

Al Ain Road; tel: 02-583 9200; usually 7.30–8.30am, Oct–Mar Thur–Fri

Lying 43km (27 miles) east of Abu Dhabi, the 10km (6-mile) course attracts camel racers from across the region. Watching the camel owners and trainers career alongside their charges in 4WDs and encouraging them on is an unforgettable sight The Camel Racing Federation is based here and the Sheikh Zayed Heritage Festival takes place in December with camel and horse racing, falconry displays and live concerts. Another camel racecourse is to be found at Al Maqam near Al Ain.

Restaurants

With fabulous fish and seafood, a range of restaurants as diverse as the cities' inhabitants and with punters boasting big appetites and hefty incomes, Dubai and Abu Dhabi provide fertile grounds for fine dining. Eating options range from *shawarma* stands to all-you-can-eat champagne brunches, and menus from some of the world's top celebrity chefs. Essentially there's a choice of two types of eating establishment: between the large, licensed hotel-restaurants, or the small, street-side independents. Head to the former for fine dining and alcohol, to the latter for culinary authenticity and unbeatable value.

DUBAI: DEIRA

Ashiana
Sheraton Dubai Creek, Baniyas Street; tel: 04-207 1733; www.sheratondubaicreek.com; Sun–Thur noon–3pm, 7.30–11.30pm, Fri–Sat 7.30–11:30pm; $$; map p.131 D1; Metro: Union Square
Even amid stiff competition from Dubai's many other fine Indian restaurants, Ashiana remains a firm local favourite. Its excellent North Indian cooking, attentive service and pleasant atmosphere with its cosy, colonial-themed interior and sitar-strumming players continue to please the punters.

The Bombay
Marco Polo Hotel, Al Muteena Street; tel: 04-272 0000; www.marcopolohotel.net; daily

Price ranges for a two-course meal with one glass of house wine (where available):
$	Dh100 or less
$$	Dh100–200
$$$	Dh200–300
$$$$	Dh300–800

12.30–3pm, 7.30pm–2am; $–$$; map p.131 D3; Metro Salah Al Din
A past winner of *Time Out*'s Best Indian award, the Bombay consistently offers flavoursome southern Indian fare at competitive prices. The location's nothing to write home about, but the service is friendly and assiduous. It's also a good option for vegetarians.

The Broadwalk
Dubai Creek Golf & Yacht Club, off Al Garhoud Road; tel: 04-295 6000; Sun–Thur noon–midnight Fri–Sat 8am–midnight, drinks served until 1am; $$; map p.134 C3
It may lie a little way southeast of town, but The Broadwalk is worth a visit for its beautiful and atmospheric setting on stilts above the Creek. You can tuck into uncomplicated but decent modern European fare whilst watching the *abras* and other boats pootle past. It's a good choice for a romantic *tête-a-tête* without blowing the

Restaurants usually open from noon to 3pm and from 7.30pm to midnight. Locals eat fairly late – usually between 8.30pm and 9pm or even later at weekends. With restaurants putting on shows (belly dancers or live music), reservations for 10pm or later are normal.

budget. For those who seeks new experiences, The Broadwalk offers the BBQ Donut (noon–9pm) where you can float on the creek in a large inflatable ring with your own barbecue on board.

China Sea
Al Maktoum Street near Clocktower roundabout; tel: 04-295 9816; daily 11am–2am; $; map p.131 E1; Metro: Deira City Centre
Winner of various local eating awards, the family-run China Sea is a treat. It stands out for its super-fresh ingredients (homemade noodles and delicious sauces), diverse dishes and novel, pick-

Left: a simple breakfast, Dubai-style.

dients and excellent value. It's also beautifully designed.

Méridien Village Terrace

Le Méridien Dubai, Airport Road; 04-702 2455; www.meridienvillageterrace-dubai.com; daily 8–11pm; $$; map p.135 D3

This outdoor restaurant is very popular with expat locals. Sat beneath twinkling fairy lights, diners can enjoy a huge themed buffet and a live band but the main draw is the good value. It's all you can eat and drink for Dh219 (regular beverages).

Reflets par Pierre Gagnaire

InterContinental Dubai, Festival City, near Garhoud Bridge; tel: 04-701 1127; www.diningdfc.com; daily 7pm–late $$$$; map p.135 D1

Taking the city (and its food awards) by storm is the new Reflets, helmed by Pierre Gagnaire, winner of three Michelin stars and ranked among the world's top 10

and-point approach, in which you select what you fancy from the raw ingredients on the shelves, and the chefs then cook it up for you. It's cheap, cheerful, fun and great value.

JW's Steakhouse

JW Marriott Hotel Dubai; Abu Baker Al Siddique Rd; tel: 04-607 7977; www.jwmarriottdubai.com; daily 5pm–midnight; $$$; map p.131 E2

With its low lighting, oak panelling and rarefied, gentleman's club-like atmosphere, JW's seems to invite you to take it seriously. You should: it's an institution among the city's carnivores, offering an impressive selection of well-cooked cuts, that range from wagyu to Aberdeen Angus and bison. It was highly commended in the *Time Out* awards Steakhouse category in 2013.

Right: JW's Steakhouse is one of the best bets for those needing nothing more than meat and two veg.

Kiku

Le Méridien Dubai, Airport Road; tel: 04-702 2455; www.kiku-dubai.com; daily 12.30–2.30pm, 6.30–11pm; $$; map p.135 D3

Sometimes the customers tell you as much about a place as its food. In Kiku's case, its perennial popularity with Japanese businessmen appears to confirm the restaurant's reputation for authenticity, artful cooking, fresh ingre-

R

Eating out in Dubai and Abu Dhabi doesn't have to break the bank. You can pick up a delicious and freshly made falafel for a couple of dirhams, a *shawarma* for under a fiver, and a cheap-and-cheerful curry for not more than a tenner. In the moderate to mid-range restaurants, main dishes go for between Dh30 to Dh50. One way to keep costs down is to head for the ethnic restaurants in the streets of Dubai's Deirha or Abu Dhabi's Al Khalidiya – the decor is basic, but the dishes are usually freshly made, more authentic and interesting than those which cater to Western customers, and sometimes a revelation. Restaurants and cafés range from Afghan to Ethiopian, Filipino to Iraqi. They don't serve alcohol, but at Dh25 upwards for what often amounts to a very ordinary glass of wine in the places that do, you may prefer to go without.

chefs. Putting to work his signature method of reinventing French classics by combining apparently contradictory ingredients, flavours and textures, the results are sensational and shockingly innovative. It's also the sheer attention to detail, the faultless service and the sumptuous surrounds that justify such a serious splurge.

Shabestan

Radisson SAS Hotel, Baniyas Road; tel: 04-222 7171; www.radissonblu.com; daily 12.30–3.15pm, Fri–Tue 7.30–11.15pm, Wed–Thur 7.30–11.30pm; $$; map p.131 C2; Metro: Union Square
An old favourite among Iranian expats, the Shabestan is considered the best Persian restau-

rant in the emirate. It also offers an atmospheric interior, views of the Creek and accomplished Iranian musicians. Don't forget to reserve a table by the window.

Table 9

Hilton Dubai Creek, Baniyas St; tel: 04-212 7551; www.table9 dubai.com; Sun–Fri 7–midnight; $$$$; map p.131 D1
Everything is made in-house but despite the attention to detail in the food, the attitude is relaxed. Diners can choose their size of portions and create a meal which suits their tastes. *Esquire* named Table 9 the Best Restaurant in the Middle East which must have pleased chefs Nick Alvis and Scott Price who took over this venue from Gordon Ramsay. Cookery classes are also available.

Thai Kitchen

Park Hyatt Dubai, Al Garhoud Road; tel: 04-317 2222; www. dubai.park.hyatt.com; Sat–Thur 7pm–midnight, Fri noon–4pm, 7pm–midnight; $$; map p.134 C3
At the centre of this slick

and stylish restaurant are two live cooking stations, where you can watch your food being freshly prepared. With a wide-ranging menu offering snack-sized portions on little plates, it's a great place to come to sample diverse dishes. The cooking's authentic, prices are competitive, and there are pretty views of the Creek.

Traiteur

Park Hyatt Dubai, off Garhoud Road; tel: 04-317 2222; www.dubai.park.hyatt.com; Friday brunch 12.30–4pm, Sun–Fri 7pm– midnight, bar Sun–Fri 6pm–midnight; $$$$; map p.134 C3
Fabulous French cuisine and slick service in warm, modern surroundings make Traiteur ideal for a special dinner or the award-winning Friday brunch.

Price ranges for a two-course meal with one glass of house wine (where available):	
$	Dh100 or less
$$	Dh100–200
$$$	Dh200–300
$$$$	Dh300–800

Left: Thai Kitchen.

BUR DUBAI

Aangan

Dhow Palace Hotel, Kuwait Street; tel: 04-359 9992; www.dhowpalacehotel.com; daily Sat–Thur, 12.30pm–3.30pm, 7pm–1am, Fri 7pm–1am; $$; map p.132 C4

A point almost of pilgrimage among Dubai's Indian expats, Aangan serves consistently high-quality North Indian fare. The interior is Moghul-inspired, and the service is hyper-attentive. There is never an empty table so it's advisable to book at weekends.

Asha's

Pyramids, Wafi Shopping Mall, Sheikh Rashid Road; tel: 04-324 4100; www.asharestaurants.com/dubai; daily 12.30–3pm, 7pm–midnight; $$; map p.134 A1; Metro Healthcare City

Though the restaurant's Indian dishes are well-rated, it's mainly the novelty value here that draws the diners. Owned by music superstar Asha Bhosle, who had a hand in the menu, it boasts a vibrant and colourful interior, a welcoming ambience and a pleasant terrace.

Khan Murjan Restaurant

Wafi Shopping Mall, Souk Ground Floor, Sheikh Rashid Road; tel: 04-327 9795; daily 10am–1am; $; map p.134 A1, Metro: Healthcare City

A previous winner of the Best Middle East and North Africa category in restaurant awards is Khan Murjan. Its winning combination of lively entertainment (including its own whirling dervishes), atmosphere (it's designed like a medieval Baghdadi souk), and diverse and delicious

Most hotel-restaurants include a 10 percent **service charge** in the bill. As the waiters very rarely see this, it's customary and kind to leave an additional something in cash. Salaries are very low, so anything that is left is greatly appreciated.

dishes covering Turkish, Egyptian and Lebanese cuisine.

Khazana

Al Nasr Leisureland; tel: 04-336 0061; www.khazana dubai.com; daily 12.30–3pm, 7–11.30pm; $$; map p.133 E2

Owned by celebrity chef Sanjeev Kapoor, the restaurant has gained a reputation for its range of flavoursome North Indian curries, baked breads and moreish 'Masala popadoms'. With its simple cane furniture and scattered pot plants, the restaurant is refreshingly unpretentious and friendly, despite its famous patron.

Lan Kwai Fong

Opposite Mövenpick Hotel, off Oud Metha Road; tel: 04-335 3680; daily noon– 3.30pm, 6.30–11.30pm; $$; map p.133 E2

The Chinese expats who crowd around the tables appear to confirm the LKF's reputation as one of the few genuine Hong Kong-style eateries in town. Authentic in decor, dishes and design, its food is excellent and the prices very reasonable. Don't miss the crispy duck, which is famous.

Lemongrass

Next to Lamcy Plaza car park, Oud Metha; tel: 04-334 2325; www.lemongrassrestaurants.com; daily noon–11.30pm; $; map p.133 D2

Multi award-winning and with a fanatical local following, the Lemongrass consistently serves superb Thai food at remarkable prices. Prepared with the freshest herbs and spices, the dishes are astonishingly aromatic and wonderfully flavoursome. Lemongrass may well turn out to be the best Thai you've ever tasted. To try Lemongrass on the run, grab a takeaway from branches at Ibn Battuta or Mirdif City Centre malls.

Medzo

Pyramids, Wafi Shopping Mall, Sheikh Rashid Road; tel: 04-324 4100; daily 12.30–3pm, 7.30–11.30pm; $$; map p.134 A1; Metro Healthcare City

With a reputation for consistently high-quality food at fair prices, plus a menu more interesting than most – Italian meets Mediterranean – Medzo has won a wide fan base. It's also unpretentious and relaxed. Medzo offers a friendly and attentive service as well as a pleasant alfresco dining option on its terrace.

TOMO

Raffles Dubai, Sheikh Rashid Road; tel: 04-357 7888; www.tomo.ae; daily 12.30–2.45pm, 6.30–11pm; $$$; map p.134 A1, Metro: Healthcare City

Voted *Time Out*'s Best Newcomer in 2013, TOMO offers delicious Japanese cuisine with stunning views across the city. Its modern elegance works equally well for a business lunch as for a romantic date.

DUBAI: JUMEIRA

La Parrilla

Jumeirah Beach Hotel, Jumeira Road, Road; tel: 04-406 8999;

www.jumeirah.com; daily 6.30pm–1am; $$$$; map p.10

Winner of *Time Out*'s Best Latin American, several years in a row, this Argentinian restaurant isn't cheap but combines famous steaks, beautifully cooked, with lovely beach views (it's on the 25th floor) and live music and dance including tango. For those seeking a sophisticated Friday brunch, La Parilla's is for adults only and it's Dh625 per head with free-flowing bubbly.

Al Mallah

Al Dhiyafah Road, Satwa; 04-398 4723; Sat–Thur 6am–4am, Fri noon–4am; $; map p.132 B1

Dhiyafah is the Arabic word for hospitality or welcome and this colourful road is worth a wander. If you get a bout of the munchies after a night out, or you just fancy something fast, cheap and cheerful, then here's the best place to head. A long-standing favourite among locals-in-the-know, the Al Mallah serves up simple but succulent and famously flavoursome chicken and lamb *shawarmas*, as well as falafel daubed with humus or tahini.

Pai Thai

Al Qasr, Madinat Jumeirah, Al Sufouh Road; tel: 04-366 6730; daily 6.30–11.30pm; $$$; map p.14

With an arrival by *abra* on the Al Qasr 'canals', followed by a candlelit dinner on the terrace with the Burj as a backdrop, and traditional musicians filling the night air, the Pai Thai is arguably the most romantic restaurant in Dubai. Offering terrific Thai dishes to boot and a

If you visit the UAE during **Ramadan**, note that everyone is expected to respect the fast whatever their religion. This means abstaining from eating, drinking (even water) and smoking in public during daylight hours; being caught doing so runs the risk of a fine. The larger hotels cater to expats through room service and sometimes also keep a restaurant open. Though finding lunch can be problematic if you're not wanting to eat in the top-end hotels (it's probably best to self-cater), Ramadan is actually a great time to visit, as the streets take on a carnival atmosphere each night with the *itfar*, the breaking of the fast, when feasting ensues, often inside tents or in restaurants which have prepared splendid buffets. Be aware that road accidents go up fairly dramatically in both cities, as ravenous and parched drivers race home at dusk. Take care driving and also crossing the city roads.

famously smooth service, the restaurant has established a well-deserved standing. Reservations are essential.

Pierchic

Al Qasr, Madinat Jumeirah, Al Sufouh Road; tel: 04-366 6730; daily 1–3pm, 7–11.30pm; $$$$; map p.14

Another sharp contender for Dubai's most romantic is Pierchic, situated on the water at the end of a pier. With stunning views of the Burj from its decked terrace, the Madinat Jumeirah and the Palm Jumeira, it's also known for the quality and consistency of both its seafood and its service. The wine list is suitably extensive also. Be sure to reserve a table on the terrace.

Right: Al Nafoorah, *see p.108.*

Pisces

Souk Madinat Jumeira, Al Sufouh Road; tel: 04-366 8888; daily noon–2.30pm, 7–11.30pm; $$$$; map p.14

Serving some of the city's finest seafood in one of its most stylish settings, Pisces boasts a firm following. All chrome, glass and blue lighting, the ambience is smooth and slick rather than romantic, but it's the food you come for. With the finest fish and seafood combined with sometimes unusual accompaniments, the cuisine in innovative and imaginative.

Al Qasr

Dubai Marine Beach Resort & Spa, Jumeira Road; tel: 04-346 1111; www.dxbmarine.com; daily 12–4pm (last food order 3.30pm), 8pm–3am (last food order 1.30am); $$; map p.10

With typical Lebanese verve and style, an evening here is more of an extravaganza than a mere meal. Well known for its excellent *mezze* and its ample grill, dinner is usually followed by live bands and a belly dancer, and diners often join in. Or you can simply sit back and puff on a *sheesha* instead.

Ravi Restaurant

Between the new mosque and Satwa roundabout, Al Satwa Rd; tel: 04-331 5353; daily 5am–3am; $; map p.132 B2

Neither chic, stylish nor beautiful, this basic Pakistani diner is yet one of the city's most beloved eating institutions. Dishing up excellent Punjabi food at unbeatable prices, it's long drawn the post-party crowd or those after

something colourful, cheap and cheerful. There's seating in or outside, but outside amid the hustle and bustle of the Satwa streets is much more fun and atmospheric.

Zheng He's

Mina A'Salaam, Madinat Jumeira, Al Sufouh Road; tel: 04-366 6730; daily noon–3pm, 7–11.30pm; $$$$; map p.14

With an interior as refined as its 'haute' Cantonese cuisine, Zheng He's is considered one of the top-ranking Asian eateries in the city. Authentic, innovative and beautifully prepared, the dishes – along with the wonderful waterside setting and superior service – make the steep prices a little easier to swallow.

Price ranges for a two-course meal with one glass of house wine (where available):	
$	Dh100 or less
$$	Dh100–200
$$$	Dh200–300
$$$$	Dh300–800

DUBAI: SHEIKH ZAYED ROAD

BICE Mare

Souk Al Bahar, Downtown Burj Dubai; tel: 04-423 0982; daily noon–midnight; $$$$; map p.12; Metro: Burj Khalifa/ Dubai Mall

This chic eatery opened in 2009 and specialises in both traditional and contemporary Italian seafood. Dishes are beautifully executed and with views of the Dubai fountains, dinner here makes for a special, if expensive, event.

The Exchange Grill

Fairmont Hotel, Sheikh Zayed Road; tel: 04-311 8316; www.fairmont.com; daily 7pm–midnight; $$$; map p.132 B1

Arguably the top steak-house in the emirate, The Exchange Grill offers a fine selection of carefully cooked cuts that rarely fail to please the city's carnivores. It also boasts a wide-ranging wine list with varieties and vintages from almost all regions. A popular place for business lunches, booking is

advised. It won best steak-house in *Time Out*'s 2013 restaurant awards.

Hoi An

Shangri-La hotel, Sheikh Zayed Road; tel: 04-405 2703; www.shangri-la.com/dubai; daily 7pm–midnight; $$

Considered the best Vietnamese restaurant in town is the Hoi An, a kind of *Indochine* (French-Vietnamese) throwback in decor and dining, complete with colonial-style ceiling fans and blue-shuttered windows. The flavours of the dishes are a fabulous French Vietnamese fusion.

Istanbul Flowers

Underneath the Safestway Supermarket, Sheikh Zayed Road; tel: 04-343 4585; www.istanbulflower.ae; daily 8.30am–1am; $

A firm favourite among the city's expat Turkish community is the Istanbul Flowers. Modest and unassuming, it serves fresh, flavoursome food, including famously succulent kebabs at rock-bot-

Friday brunch is a hallowed institution in Dubai and Abu Dhabi. The equivalent of a Saturday brunch in the West, it marks the end of the working week, the beginning of the weekend, and an attempt to recover after the excesses of the night before, even if that means applying 'the hair of the dog' to the extreme: taking full advantage of the unlimited wine or champagne that's often included in the 'deal'. Most self-respecting hotel-restaurants put on a buffet, each more lavish than the last as they battle to bring in the punters – brunch is a lucrative market. If you want to give it a go, perhaps after an appetite-inducing swim in the sea, head for Dubai's beautiful hotel Al Qasr *(see p.74)* in Madinat Jumeira. With its gorgeous terrace setting, top-notch food that ranges from oysters and crab to wagyu beef and *foie gras*, it won *Time Out's* Best Friday Brunch three years running. 2013's Best Brunch went to Bubbalicious at the Westin *(see p.78)*. For an outstanding Asian-style brunch, try the Thai Kitchen *(see p.104)*, which lets you sample almost the restaurant's entire menu. Top brunches are not cheap (Dh350 or more), but as a quintessential Dubai/Abu Dhabi experience, they're memorable.

tom prices. There's also a branch at Healthcare City (tel: 04-449 5330).

Al Nafoorah

Emirates Towers, Sheikh Zayed Road; tel: 04-319 8079; www.jumeirah.com; Sun–Thur 12.30–3.30pm, Fri–Sat 1–3.30pm, daily 7pm–midnight; $$; map p.12; Metro: Emirates Towers
Serving outstanding Lebanese food in its ele-

gant, restrained and somewhat formal interior, Al Nafoorah is a popular choice for business lunches and counts among its customers Sheikh Mo himself. There is a small terrace outside with a fountain (after which the restaurant is named) in the shadow of the Sheikh Zayed strip. The 'Al Nafoorah grill' is the speciality – five mixed seafood and meat skewers served to look like a sun.

The Noodle House

The Boulevard, Emirates Towers, Ground Level, Sheikh Zayed Road; tel: 04-319 8088; www.thenoodlehouse.com; daily noon–midnight; $$; map p.12; Metro: Emirates Towers
A kind of Southeast-Asian version of Wagamama, with long, shared tables and benches and an informal service and atmosphere, the ever-popular Noodle House serves a wide selection of tasty Asian appetisers, plus soup, noodle, rice and wok dishes (from crispy duck wontons to bakmi goring) at good prices.

There are also branches at the Souk Madinat Jumeira, the Dubai Marina Mall, in the Burjuman Shopping Centre, in the base of the DIFC Gate and at the Gloria Hotel, Media City.

Options

Dubai International Convention Tower, Dubai World Trade Centre, off Sheikh Zayed Road; tel: 04-329 3293; www.options dubai.com; daily noon–3pm,

Left: Vu's – the clue is in the name.

the ostrich-leather table-cloths), it's a popular place for a business lunch, and the service is no less immaculate.

DUBAI MARINA

BiCE

Hilton Dubai Jumeirah, Dubai Marina; tel: 04-318 2520; daily 12.30pm–11.30pm; $$$$; map p.14

The Dubai version of the well-established Milanese chain is ranked by Italian expats as one of the city's best Italian restaurants and remains ever-popular. The dishes are classic North Italian executed perfectly, but it's not cheap.

Eauzone

One&Only Royal Mirage; tel: 04-399 9999; www.royal mirage.oneandonlyresorts.com; daily noon–3.30pm, 7–11.30pm; $$$; map p.14

Another keen contender for most romantic restaurant in Dubai is Eauzone. Set on a wooden jetty above the illuminated, lagoon-like pool of the One&Only, it serves up sublime Asian-fusion food using the finest ingredients and preparation. Reserve a table on the jetty. Lunchtime is a far more casual affair.

Indego by Vineet

Grosvenor House, West Marina Beach; tel: 04-399 8888; www.grosvenorhouse-dubai.

7–11.30pm; $$; map p.132 B1
Decorated like a kind of Bollywood boudoir, this Indian restaurant is owned by celebrity chef Sanjeev Kapoor. Like the decor, the dishes dazzle with stunning Mogul-like combinations of spices, nuts, herbs and citrus fruits. The range of desserts are also popular among its many customers.

Rivington Grill

Souk Al Bahar, Downtown Burj Dubai; tel: 04 423 0903; www.rivingtongrill.ae; daily noon–11pm; $$$; map p.12; Metro: Burj Khalifa/ Dubai Mall
Catering to homesick British expats, Rivington Grill is well-known for serving the best fish and chips in Dubai. Despite its flair for tackling traditional British comfort cuisine, it also caters to more sophisticated diners. Rivington Grill remains a classy affair. It overlooks the Dubai Fountains and the service is excellent. Lunch here is good value. There is also a

Left: Ossiano, *see p.110.*

---

branch at Madinat Jumeira (tel: 04-366 6464) and an attached bar, Rivi Bar.

Teatro

Towers Rotana Hotel, Sheikh Zayed Road; tel: 04-343 8000; daily 6–11.30pm; $$
A firm fixture on the restaurant scene for over eight years, Teatro keeps its customers by offering high-quality international dishes from a wide range of places: Europe, India, China and Southeast Asia; great for groups who can't agree on where to dine. At the weekends in particular it's lively and fun.

Vu's

50th Floor, Emirates Towers, Sheikh Zayed Road; tel: 04-319 8088; www.jumeirah.com; Sun–Thur 12.30–3pm, Sun–Fri 7.30pm–midnight; $$$; map p.12; Metro: Emirates Towers
Though it's the gob-smacking view from the 50th floor over the Sheikh Zayed strip that is the main draw, the haute cuisine can be no less dizzying. Slick, smart and stylish (down to

---

Price ranges for a two-course meal with one glass of house wine (where available):	
$	Dh100 or less
$$	Dh100–200
$$$	Dh200–300
$$$$	Dh300–800

com; daily 12.30pm–3pm, Fri–Wed 7pm–midnight, Thur 7pm–1am; Fri–Sat brunch 12.30pm–4pm; $$$; map p.14

Helmed by Vaneet Bhatia, one of India's first chefs to be awarded a Michelin star, Indego's dishes reflect its master's distinct signature style: combining Asian and European ingredients, preparation and techniques. The results are innovative and startling, and have established Indego as one of Dubai's top Indian eateries.

Ossiano

Atlantis Palm Hotel, Palm Jumeirah; tel: 04-426 2626; www.atlantisthepalm.com; daily 7pm–midnight; $$$$; map p.14

The late top Spanish chef, Santi Santamaria set up this restaurant (his first outside Spain) and Ossiano ranks among the best – and most expensive – seafood restaurants in the city. The Catalan-influenced cooking is superb, with dishes carefully conceived and beautifully executed. There's also a terrific wine list, though prices may quickly quell your thirst. However the food almost takes second stage to the breathtaking venue; dramatic and stunning with tables set next to the Ambassador lagoon.

Ottomans

Grosvenor House Hotel, Al Sufouh Road; tel: 04-399 8888;

www.grosvenorhouse-dubai.com; Tue–Sun 7.30pm–1am; $$$; map p.14

Superb food, a pleasant terrace, and belly dancers prove to be a winning combination. *Time Out* voted this to be the city's best Middle Eastern and African restaurant in 2013.

Rhodes Mezzanine

Grosvenor House Hotel, West Marina Beach, Al Sufouh Road; tel: 04-399 8888; Mon–Sat 7pm–11.30pm; $$$; map p.14

The decor may be a bit eclectic, colourful and far-fetched, but the cooking's spot on. Overseen by celebrity British chef Gary Rhodes, old British faves are reborn, but burst with fabulous flavours, the freshest of ingredients and careful execution. Given the quality of the cuisine, the prices are not excessive.

Tagine

One&Only Royal Mirage, Al Sufouh Road; tel: 04-399 9999; Tue–Sun 7–11.30pm; $$; map p.14

Moroccan eatery Tagine is styled like a *riad* restaurant from Marrakesh, complete with monumental entrance door, a candle-lined area beckoning you in, and the feast-for-all-the-senses experience, with live music, wafting incense, as well as enticing food. The food's not the finest in the city, but it's the atmosphere and fun you come for here.

ABU DHABI: CORNICHE

BiCE

Jumeirah at Etihad Towers, Podium Level 1, ; www.bice group.com; tel: 02 811 5666; daily noon–3pm, 7–11pm; $$$; map p.136 A3

The well-respected

Milanese chain has spawned an Abu Dhabi version, which is ranked both as one of the best Italian restaurants and also best venue for a business lunch. With a top-notch Italian chef combining the freshest and best local ingredients with specialised items imported from Italy, the cuisine is authentic, imaginative and flavoursome. The decor is classic but chic; in the evening, low lighting creates a more intimate atmosphere.

Chamas

InterContinental Abu Dhabi, Bainunah Street, Khor Al Bateen; tel: 02-666 6888; daily 6–11.30pm, bar 6pm–1am, Fri brunch noon–4pm; $$$; map p.136 B2

A big hit locally is Chamas, designed like a Brazilian *churrascaria*, and a carnivore's dream. For a set price (Dh315 per person, includes soft drinks), p*assadores* ('Brazilian' waiters) bring freshly barbecued beef, lamb, chicken, offal and sausages to diners at

Price ranges for a two-course meal with one glass of house wine (where available):	
$	Dh100 or less
$$	Dh100–200
$$$	Dh200–300
$$$$	Dh300–800

110

their tables – and go on doing so until they're told to stop (via a simple token placed to the table and turned to red or green). Hot veggies are also brought round, and there's a huge crescent-shaped salad bar. Live Latin bands and samba dancers add to the lively party atmosphere. Go hungry.

Hakkasan

Emirates Palace, Corniche Street West, Ras Al Akhdar; tel:02-690 7999; www. hakkasan.com/abu-dhabi; daily 6pm–midnight; Fri–Sat noon–3pm, bar 6pm–2am; $$$$; map p.136 A3

Designer bar, lounge and restaurant, nowhere else in Abu Dhabi serves exquisite Chinese cuisine in surroundings as stylish. It opened in Abu Dhabi in

2010, bringing a taste of the flagship restaurant in London.

Lebanese Flower

Nr Choithram Supermarket, off 26th Street, Al Khalidiyah; tel: 02-665 8700; daily 7.30am–3am; $; map p.136 B2

A long-standing favourite locally, the Lebanese Flower offers fresh, authentic and delicious Lebanese dishes at unbeatable prices. It may be no-frills and basic, but it's fast, efficient and never disappoints. The *mezze*, meat dishes, falafel and fruit juices are all highly rated by the regulars.

Marakesh

Mezzanine Floor, Millennium Hotel, Khalifa Bin Zayed Street, Al Markaziyah; tel: 02-626 7334; daily 7pm–3am; $–$$; map p.137 D3

Though offering one of the most reasonably priced nights outs in town, the Marakesh doesn't hold back. Its decor is pink and plush, its dishes wide-ranging (including Lebanese options) and generous, and

its entertainment extravagant: live bands and a belly dancer. The atmosphere is outstanding.

Porto Bello

Grand Millennium Al Wahda, Hazza Bin Zayed Street, Al Wahda Complex; tel: 02-495 3905; daily noon–11.30pm; $$; map p.137 D1

A newcomer which wows with its faultless classic Italian cooking. The setting is nothing special but the manner in which flavours are combined and the skills in the kitchen are more than enough to merit a visit. The pasta here is simply perfect.

Tiara

36th Floor, Marina Mall, Breakwater, West Corniche; tel: 02-681 9090; daily noon–midnight; $$; map p.136 B3

Newly opened Tiara sits atop a 126m (328ft) tower, in a glass-clad floor that revolves, giving guests stunning panoramic views of the city during their meal. With a stated aim of serving top-class cuisine (Southwest France-inspired) at reasonable rates, it offers terrific value and an experience to remember. Tiara is also open for lunch and tea.

Vasco's

Hilton International Abu Dhabi, Al Khubeirah; tel: 02-681 1900; daily noon–3.30pm, 7–11pm; $$–$$$; map p.136 B1

Offering spacious alfresco dining on the waterfront, an international menu which ranges from Italian and Arabic to Asian (perfect for couples or families who can't agree), and a reputation for good-quality food at affordable prices, Vasco's is

an old favourite locally. Reservations are advised.

Wasabi

Al Diar Mina Hotel, Meena Road, Al Markaziyah; tel: 02-678 1000; daily noon–3pm, 6pm–11pm; $; map p.137 D3
With its bright, uncluttered interior, booths with sliding doors complete with complimentary slippers, the little Wasabi could come straight out of downtown Tokyo. Dishes range from fabulous sushi (considered the city's best) to sublime seafood, fish, meat, noodle and rice dishes. With its combination of authenticity and fresh and flavoursome food served at outstanding prices, the Wasabi attracts a fervent local following.

Price ranges for a two-course meal with one glass of house wine (where available):	
$	Dh100 or less
$$	Dh100–200
$$$	Dh200–300
$$$$	Dh300–800

CENTRAL & SOUTH ABU DHABI

Bord Eau

Shangri-La hotel, Bain Al Jesrain; tel: 02-509 8888; daily 7–11.30pm; $$–$$$; map p.20
Ranked as the best French restaurant in the emirate, Bord Eau is also one of its most romantic. In style, the spacious interior is opulent Art Deco, the food modern French (with many ingredients imported especially from France). Offering superb cuisine at remarkably reasonable prices, unusually knowledgeable and passionate staff, and an intimate atmosphere, it's well worth a visit. It was *Time Out*'s Restaurant of the Year in 2012.

Finz

Beach Rotana Hotel & Towers, off 10th Street, Tourist Club Area; tel: 02-697 9011; daily 12.30pm–3.30pm, 7pm–11.30pm; $$$; map p.137 E2
Considered by some as the city's finest seafood restaurant, it's also one of its most romantic, particularly during the winter when you can dine on the decked terrace overlooking the water. The Finz's interior is designed like a semi-open-sided chalet and you can watch the live kitchen station at work on one side and the ocean views on the other. With outstanding seafood served with a slight Asian slant, a great setting and a relaxed ambience, it makes a memorable evening.

Hoi An

Shangri-La hotel, Bain Al Jesrain; tel: 02-509 8888; daily 6pm–11.30pm; $$–$$$; map p.20
With its neo-colonial decor and classic Vietnamese food with a modern take, the award-winning Hoi An is popular for its sheer quality, creativity and imagination. With a lovely terrace for the winter months and service that is both knowledgeable and attentive, it makes a great place for a relaxed dinner.

India Palace

As Salaam Street, Al Meena; tel: 02-644 8777; www.india palace.ae; daily noon–midnight; $; map p.137 D3

One of the city's most popular Indian restaurants, it's also one of its most reasonable. Packed to the rafters at the weekends, it's atmospheric, fun and lively. If you're looking for a more romantic dinner *à deux*, you can head for one of the little booths upstairs. The North Indian dishes are authentic, freshly made and excellent, though beware that 'hot' means hot. Decorwise it's nothing fancy, but it's the good food at great prices that's the main attraction. There are branches at Mazyad Mall and Mushrif Mall.

Noodle House

Al Wahdah Mall, Sheikh Hazza Bin Zayed Street; tel: 02-443 7391; Sat–Wed noon–11pm,

Left: Bord Eau.

Thur–Fri noon–midnight; $; map p.137 D1

A kind of Southeast Asian version of Wagamama, with long, shared tables and benches and an informal service and atmosphere, the ever-popular Noodle House serves a diverse selection of tasty Asian appetisers, plus soup, noodle, rice and wok dishes (from crispy duck wontons to bakmi goring) at good prices. There's also a branch in Souk Qaryat Al Beri.

Rodeo Grill

Beach Rotana Hotel & Towers, off 10th Street, Tourist Club; tel: 02-697 9011; www.rotana.com; daily 12.30pm– 3.30pm, 7–11.30pm; $$$–$$$$; map p.137 E2

Abu Dhabi's first steakhouse, Rodeo Grill continues to pull in the punters with its fine selection of choice cuts, from wagyu to Aberdeen Angus and bison, as well as some excellent seafood and desserts. With its wooden

interior and classic, green leather armchairs, it's fine dining American-style.

Tarbouche al Basha

Souk Central Market, World Trade Center, Al Markaziyah; tel: 02-628 2220; daily 10am–1am; $; map p.137 D3

The focus of this Lebanese rooftop garden restaurant's cooking is simplicity and freshness. Delicious kebabs and grills are the order of the day and for the price, it's hard to find a better atmosphere.

Ushna

Souk Qaryat Al Beri, Bain Al Jessrain; tel: 02-558 1769; daily 12.30pm–6pm, Sun–Thur 7–11.30pm, Fri brunch noon–4pm, Fri–Sat 7pm–12.30am; $$$

With its stunning views of the Grand Mosque and the Maqtaa Creek, Ushna makes for a romantic and sophisticated spot. Children below three years are not allowed. Locals rave about the Indian cuisine and the terrace is very popular for soaking up the atmosphere.

Right: Hoi An.

113

Shopping

Shopping is for many Dubai and Abu Dhabi's main draw. They boast more malls per square kilometre than any two cities on earth. With no expense spared to lure in the shoppers, the malls have become attractions in their own right, with facilities that can beggar belief. Playing a key social role, they also offer great insights into the cities' psyche. On the reverse side of the coin are the city's souks. Though no match for the bazaars of some Arab cities like Marrakech, a visit is a must, particularly at night when they're most active, colourful and vibrant. Along with the Armani and Prada, you may well be packing silk, spices and gold.

BARGAINING

Love it or loathe it, bargaining is an integral part of the traditional souk experience. The secret is to keep it light-hearted and fun. The system goes something like this: the vendor proposes a price, the buyer halves it, and eventually the two meet somewhere in between. Once you've started haggling, you're expected to buy, and once you've shaken on a deal, you're expected to pay up. In the malls, prices in most chain stores are fixed. Bargaining is really reserved for the souks only but it's worth asking anywhere if you are getting the 'best price'.

CARPETS/FURNISHINGS

DUBAI

Al Orooba Oriental
Burjuman Centre, Sheikh Khalifa bin Zayed Road; tel: 04-351 0919; Sat–Thur 10am– 10pm, Fri 2–10pm; map p.130 B1; Metro: Khalid Bin Al Waleed
A long-time fave with expats, the Al Orooba is a true Aladdin's cave of

Above: bartering is expected at all souks and markets.

high-quality carpets and kilims, as well as antique silver (including *khanjars* – the traditional curved knives), Bedouin jewellery, ceramics and embroidery.

Pride of Kashmir
Deira City Centre, off Baniyas Road; tel: 04-295 0655; daily 10am–10pm; map p.134 D4
Renowned for its beautiful Kashmiri and Persian silk carpets – you'll be spoilt for choice. Also wide-ranging are the more rustic-looking kilims and rugs from Turkey and Central Asia. The store is also

known for its high-quality pashminas sold at competitive prices, as well as decorative home items. There are also branches at Souk Madinat Jumeira and Souk Al Bahar.

ABU DHABI

Carpet Souk
off Al Meena Road, Al Meena; Sun–Thur, Sat 10am–6pm; Fri 2–10pm; map p.137 E3
Don't judge by appearances: the souk (also known as Afghan Souk) is still the best place to pick up a bargain, though you may have to sift through the machine-mades from China and India. Gems from Iran and Kashmir lurk deep inside the store, if you ask to see them.

ELECTRONICS

Abu Dhabi and particularly Dubai offer among widest choice and best-priced

For clothing, *see Fashion, p.56–9*; for beauty products, *see Pampering, p.97*, for food, *see Food and Drink , p.64–5.*

Merchants have long traded **carpets** in Dubai. With carpets coming from Iran, as well as Pakistan, Turkey and Central Asia, and sold at tax-free prices, Dubai and Abu Dhabi are great places to buy them. Quality varies from exquisite pieces to lurid, shag-pile monstrosities. But if you take your time, determine your budget, ask to see 'the best quality', and bargain hard, you may well come away with a corker. A high density of knots per square inch indicates quality. Many shops in Dubai can produce DCCI (Dubai Chamber of Commerce & Industry) certificates of authenticity.

Most malls open from 10am to 10pm Sunday to Wednesday and from 10am to midnight Thur–Sat.

electronic goods of anywhere outside East Asia.

DUBAI

Beside the electronic chain shops found in the malls, you may want to check out the often rock-bottom prices on the street, particularly Bur Dubai's so-called **Computer Street** (the shops surrounding Khalid bin Al Waleed Road), as well as **Electrical Street** next to the Textile Souk on Al Fahidi Street, also in Bur Dubai.

Al Ain Centre

Al Mankhool Road; tel: 04-352 6663; www.alaincentre.com; Sat–Thur 10am–2.30pm, 4.30–10pm, Fri 2.20–10pm; map p.130 B1

Also known as the 'Computer Plaza' and one of the best places to pick up bargains, with over 60 independent retail stores.

Carrefour

Deira City Centre, off Baniyas Road; tel: 800-732 32; www.carrefouruae.com; Sat–Wed 9am–midnight, Thur–Fri 9am–1am; map p.134 C4

Carrefour is known to offer some of the best bargains in the city. Electronics include digital cameras, mobile phone iPods and laptops. There are also branches at Mall of the Emirates and Mirdif City Centre.

Jumbo Electronics

Deira City Centre; tel: 04-295 3915; www.jumbocorp.com; Sun–Wed 10am–10pm, Thur–Sat 10am–midnight; map p.134 C4

Jumbo is one of the biggest distributors of Japanese electronics in the world. Staff are also helpful and more knowledgeable than in some stores. There are nearly 20 outlets spread across the city including Mall of the Emirates and Mirdif City Centre; check on the website to find your nearest store.

GOLD AND GEMS

Boasting well over 1,000 jewellery shops between them, Abu Dhabi and Dubai offer a quantity, quality and variety of jewellery rarely seen elsewhere. With minimal or zero tax on imports and sales, plus fierce competition between shops, prices are low.

DUBAI

Deira Gold Souk

Off, Sikkat Al Khail Street, Deira; map p.130 B3

There's probably nowhere on Earth where you'll see such an undiluted density of gold. Even if you've no intention of buying, a visit here is a must. Shop windows positively drip with displays of minutely decorated gold bangles, multi-tiered necklaces and fantastic face-pieces much-beloved by Arab and Asian brides (look out for them window-shopping).

Gold and Diamond Park

Sheikh Zayed Road, between Interchange 3 and 4; tel: 04-362 7777; www.goldanddiamond

115

park.com; Sun–Thur 10am–10pm, Sat–Fri 10am–midnight; Metro First Gulf Bank

Slightly off the beaten-track, the Park sees fewer tourists than in Deira, but more serious gem-shoppers. This is the place to come for diamonds at astonishing prices. Other gemstones can also be found, as well as some all-gold and platinum jewellery.

ABU DHABI

Gold Centre

Madinat Zayed Shopping Centre; 4th Street, Madinat Zayed; tel: 02-633 3311; www.madinat zayed-mall.com; daily Sat–Fri 9am–11pm; map p.137 D2

It may not share the same spectacular scale as Dubai's gold souks, but the centre still merits a visit and offers comparable quality and prices.

MALLS

In the UAE, malls are not just a place to shop, they're a way of life. A visit to experience mall culture is a must. Here's a quick guide.

DUBAI

Deira City Centre (off Floating Bridge; www.deiracitycentre. com; map.134 C4) has its own metro station, a good variety of shops which range from high-street clothes stores such as Debenhams,

---

A souk or souq is the Arabic word for open-air marketplace and the traditional ones in Dubai are a fascinating combination of tourist trap and something more enduring. If you don't see one of the old souks (Textile, Spice or Gold) in Dubai it's an experience missed. Souk opening times vary; there's no hard-and-fast rule. In general, souk shops open Sat–Thur from between 8–10am to 1pm and 4–7pm or later, and Fri from 4–7pm or later. Some remain open all day. Some may find the grimy, busy environment and the haggling required in the old souks intimidating but there's still the chance to get a taste of the souk atmosphere in the gorgeous, if a little sterile, replica souks to be found in Wafi (Khan Murjan), next to Dubai Mall (Souk Al Bahar) and at the Souk Madinat.

---

to jewellery, book and electronic stores. **Festival City Mall** (off Business Bay crossing bridge; www.festivalcity.com; map p.135 D1) occupies an attractive spot right on the Creek. It contains IKEA and its great-value café and Marks and Spencer as well as plenty of alfresco eating outlets which overlook a manmade canal. **Mirdif City Centre** (off Festival City Road; www.mirdifcitycentre.com) has transformed sleepy suburb Mirdif into a shop-

pers' dream. It has 430 stores and great activities for children of all ages. **Dubai Mall** (off Doha Street; www.thedubaimall.com), one of the largest malls, also offers some the city's best attractions including a giant aquarium, an ice rink and the Dubai Fountains. This also has its own metro station on Sheikh Zayed Road but be prepared to then get on a feeder bus which takes you to the mall. **Dubai Outlet Mall** (Al Ain Road; www.dubaioutlet mall.com) is worth the 20-minute taxi ride for the heavily-discounted designer and high-street labels, as well as electronics. **Ibn Battuta Mall** (Sheikh Zayed Road; www. ibnbattutamall.com) one of Dubai's most mammoth, offers a large range of international high-street names that you can trawl as you travel the themed worlds. **Mall of the Emirates** (Sheikh Zayed Road; www. malloftheemirates.com) boasts over 400 outlets including UAE's own Harvey Nichols, it's so big that mall walking is an organised form of exercise *(see box, p.15)*. It also offers some of the best experiences including Ski Dubai (where you can hit the slopes after the shops), luxury cinema seats, and kid-pleasing activities *(see p.14)*. **Souk Madinat Jumeira** (Jumeira Road; www.madinatjumeirah.com) is designed like a traditional souk and has a good blend of boutiques, galleries and food shops as well as containing some of the city's most popular bars, cafés, restaurants and nightspots. **The Village** (Jumeira Road; www.thevillagedubai.com)

Left: Gold Souk.

Right: traditional footwear.

offers the most original and unusual boutique stores in the city. **Wafi Shopping Mall** (Sheikh Rashid Road; www.wafi.com; map p.134 A1) is egyptian-themed and one of Dubai's most exclusive malls housing major labels and names. **Boulevard** (Sheikh Zayed Road; www.boulevarddubai.com) offers a range of popular bars, cafés and restaurants as well as a range of top-designer names including Chloé and Juicy Couture.

ABU DHABI

Abu Dhabi Mall (off 2nd Street; www.abudhabi-mall.com; map p.137 E2) boasts over 200 outlets and a good range of restaurants as well as cinemas. **Madinat Zayed Shopping Centre** (East Road; map p.137 D2) is home to 400 outlets. **Al Wahda Mall** (Sheikh Hazza bin Zayed Street; www.alwahda-mall.com; map p.137 D1), a recent arrival, is popular for its large range of international high-street stores in its light and sunny interior. **Marina Mall** (Breakwater; www.marina mall.ae; map p.136 B3) stretches over 120,000 sq m and incorporates over 400 outlets including top designer names, restaurants and cafés, an ice rink, a 9-screen cinema and a bowling alley.

SPICES AND PERFUMES

DUBAI

Ajmal
Bur Juman Centre, off Sheikh Khalifa bin Zayed Road; tel: 04-351 5505; www.ajmal perfume.com; Sat–Thur 10am–10pm, Fri 2–10pm
Much loved locally for its *attars* (Arabic-style per-

fumes made from essential oils), Ajmal can blend one for you in-house. Branches are also at DCC, Mirdif CC, Mall of the Emirates and Dubai Mall.

Spice Souk
Off Old Baladiya Street, Deira; map p.130 B2
Located in narrow arcades hung with old wrought-iron lanterns, the Spice Souk is one of the most atmospheric spots in the city. Less than a century ago it comprised several hundred stalls; today only a trace remains. It's the perfect place to buy Iranian saffron (from Dh5 – a fraction of the price back home) or maybe some *za'atar*, the Arabian mixed herb and spice condiment used since medieval times.

ABU DHABI

Ajmal
Abu Dhabi Mall, 10th Street; tel: 02-645 7060; www.ajmal perfume.com; Sat–Thur 10am–10pm, Fri 2–10pm; map p.137 E2
Apothecary-like, with rows of bottles containing precious essence oils, this traditional Arab *parfumerie* can blend to order. Some of the scent bottles are beautifully ornate.

DUBAI

Al Jaber Gallery
Mall of the Emirates, Sheikh Zayed Road; tel: 04-341 4103; Sun–Wed 10am–10pm, Thur–Sat 10am–midnight
Al Jaber is a treasure trove of Arabian arts and crafts including textiles, jewellery and rugs.

Camel Company
Dubai Mall tel: 04-388 4559; www.camelcompany.ae; Sun–Wed 10am–10pm, Thur–Sat 10am–midnight
If you're after the classic furry-camel souvenir, here's your shop. Camels come on everything from coffee cups to mouse pads.

Golden Arrows Novelties
Bur Dubai Souk; tel: 04-353 8446; Sun–Thur 9.30am–1.30pm, 4.30–9.30pm; map p.130 B2
The tiny but cavernous Golden Arrows stocks quite a good collection of antiques including *khanjars*, swords, coins, Bedouin jewellery and coffee pots.

Showcase Antiques, Art & Frames
Jumeira Road, Umm Suqeim; tel: 04-348 8797; Sat–Thur 9am–8pm
A favourite spot of expats, the Showcase boasts an unrivalled collection of high-quality and authenticated traditional antiques.

ABU DHABI

Khalifa Centre
Near Abu Dhabi Mall, 10th Street; tel: 02-667 9900; daily 10am–10pm; map p.137 E2
This colourful artisanal mall sells everything from *shisha* sets to Bedouin jewellery and high-quality rugs.

Sports

With unlimited sunshine, warm waters, kilometres of beach, and sports facilities that rank among the best in the world, Dubai and Abu Dhabi are great places to get active. Or at least to work up a sweat or an appetite before sidling back to the spa or dinner table. Both cities are particularly known for their near-perfect golf courses and fine equestrian facilities. Few cities offer such a wide range of water sports either. With first-class equipment and well-trained instructors, it's a good place to learn. For desert sports and activities, *see Desert Excursions, p.44–7*; for four-footed spectator sports, *see Racing, p.98–101*.

ADVENTURE SPORT COMPANIES

ABU DHABI

Arabian Adventures
Mezzanine Floor, Emirates Travel Shop, Corniche Road; tel: 02-691 1711; www.arabian-adventures.com; Sat–Thur 9am–6pm; map p.136 B3
If you're keen to escape the city, the company offers well-organised 'desert safaris', including into the famous Empty Quarter. The standard tours may be too tame and civilised for some, but they also custom-make tours, as well as renting reliable 4WDs (with or without drivers).

FISHING

DUBAI

Art Marine
Pavilion Sports Centre, Jumeirah Beach Hotel, Jumeira Road; tel: 04-348 1281; www.artmarine.net; daily 7am–6pm
One of the biggest fishing outfits in the region, Art Marine rents boats for six to

Above: hire a 4WD and driver unless you have off-roading experience.

12 people with full fishing gear (and bait) provided.

ABU DHABI

Arabian Divers and Sportfishing Charters
Ground Floor, Marina Al Bateen Resort, Bainuna Street, near UAE Central Bank; tel: 050-614 6931; www.fishabudhabi.com; Sat–Thur 8am–9pm, Fri 9am–4pm; map p.136 A2
This firm offers big game fishing, light tackle fishing and stand up fishing as well as sightseeing boat charters.
Blue Dolphin Company

InterContinental Hotel, off Bainunah Street; tel: 02-666 6888; www.interconti.com; Sat–Thur 9am–6pm; map p.136 B2
Blue Dolphin offers boats, equipment and instruction for both line and trawl fishing. Catches can include barracuda, hammour, jacks, kingfish and dorado, and sometimes tuna, sailfish and queenfish too. September to April is the best time to go fishing in the Gulf.

GOLF

With ever more courses appearing (Dubai's much-anticipated, Greg Norman-designed The Earth among them) and fine weather, the UAE is working hard to position itself as the world's top golfing destination. For more information on golf in Dubai, check out: www.dubaigolf.com.

DUBAI

Dubai Creek Golf & Yacht Club
Opposite Deira City Centre Mall, near Floating Bridge, Al Garhoud; tel: 04-295 6000;

Left: meanwhile, it could be 43°C (109°F) outside.

golfer Colin Montgomerie of Ryder Cup fame, the club stretches over 80 hectares (200 acres) and includes no fewer than 14 lakes and 72 bunkers, as well as the 'famous 13th' – reputedly the largest single piece of green in the world and measuring in at 5,394 sq m (58,000 sq ft). Among its many facilities are an academy, a high-tech 'swing studio' and putting greens.

ABU DHABI

Abu Dhabi Golf Club by Sheraton

Tel: 02-558 8990; www.adgolfclub.com; daily 6am–sunset; admission charge
Host of the international Abu Dhabi Golf Championship, the ADGC's world-class facilities include two par-72 18-hole courses, pitching and putting greens and a good academy.

HORSE RIDING

Kings of the Gulf's equestrian world, Dubai and Abu Dhabi boast some of the finest bloodstock on Earth.

DUBAI

Desert Palm Riding School

On Al Awir Road, past Dragonmart; www.desertpalm.peraquum.com; tel: 050-451 7773; opening times vary; admission charge
Set in the grounds of a boutique hotel and an exclusive gated residential area, Desert Palm has its own polo pitches. Riding a horse or watching a polo match on their beautiful lawns seems a world away from the desert close by.

Part of the Dubailand project which has gone ahead *(see Architecture, p.28)*, and the drive to bring the world's most important sporting events to the city, is the new **Dubai Sport City**. Boasting three stadiums – the largest with a capacity of 60,000 and 'convertible' in function, depending on the sport it's hosting – it hopes to attract major international events in the future, including the ICC Cricket World Cup and the Hockey World Cup.

---

www.dubaigolf.com; daily 7am–6pm; admission charge; map p.134 C3
Though ranking among the world's top clubs, the stunningly designed, par-71 championship course is open to outsiders (who hold a valid handicap certificate). Facilities also include a golf academy (where beginners can take classes), and the Dubai Creek iconic clubhouse.

Emirates Golf Club

Interchange No.5, Sheikh Zayed Road; tel: 04-380 1234;

www.dubaigolf.com; daily 7am–6pm; admission charge
Host of the annual Dubai Desert Classic, and the first fully grass course in the Middle East, the Emirates is something of an institution. Facilities include two 18-hole championship courses (one redesigned by Nick Faldo in 2006), two driving ranges and the Peter Cowen Golf Academy.

Al Badia Golf Club

Al Rebat Street, Festival City; tel: 04-601 0101; www.albadiagolfclub.ae; daily 6am–sundown; admission charge
Designed by famous, US, golf-course architect Robert Trent Jones II, the new 18-hole championship Al Badia course is the jewel in the crown of this complex, which also includes a golfing academy.

Montgomerie

Emirates Hills, off Interchange 5, Sheikh Zayed Road; tel: 04-390 5600; www.themontgomerie.com; 6.30am–sundown; admission charge
Designed by Scottish

119

Emirates Equestrian Centre

Beyond Endurance Village, follow signs from Al Ain Road, exit 37 Lisali or from Al Barsha Road, near Bab Al Shams hotel; tel: 050-558 7656; www.emiratesequestriancentre.com; mid-Sept–mid-June lessons daily 7–11am, 4–7pm; admission charge

Part of the huge equestrian scene in the UAE is the EEC, considered one of the leading riding schools in the Gulf. It offers lessons in dressage, showjumping and eventing by single or batch lessons. Facilities include nearly 200 horses, 12 arenas, a cross-country course and trial rides.

Jebel Ali Horse Riding

Jebel Ali Golf Resort & Spa; tel: 04-814 5555; www.jaresorts hotels.com; stables open daily Oct–June 7am–noon, 4–7pm, summer 6–8am, 6–8pm; admission charge

If the idea of a canter across the desert appeals, this is the place. For novices, there's a paddock and fully qualified instruction at hand.

ABU DHABI

Abu Dhabi Equestrian Club

Off 19th Street, Al Mushriff; tel: 02-445 55500; www.adec-web.com; Sat–Thur 7am–7pm; admission charge

The hub of Abu Dhabi's active horse-racing scene, the club also gives classes in riding, showjumping and polo. The stables boast over 100 horses and facilities for showjumping.

MOTOR RACING AND KARTING

Dubai Autodrome

Off Interchange 4, Sheikh Zayed Road; tel: 04-367 8700; www.

dubaiautodrome.com; opening times vary; admission charge

Fit for Formula One (which it may one day host), this amazing 5.39km (3⅓ mile) circuit boasts a reputable race and driving school, as well as a very popular and equally well-designed, CIK-sanctioned kart track measuring 1.2km (¾ mile). The 390cc 'pro-karts' reach speeds of up to 100kmph (62mph). The Autodrome also has karts and tracks for kids.

ABU DHABI

Yas Marina Circuit

Yas Island; tel: 02-659 9800; www.yasmarinacircuit.com; admission charge

A dazzling Formula 1 track opened in the city in October 2009. Home to the annual Abu Dhabi Grand Prix, it measures 5.55km (3.4 miles) and has 21 turns; 12 left and 9 right. It also hosts some of the world's top motor racing series.

In addition to hosting some of the world's top sporting events Dubai also sees a few home-sprung varieties. If you're tired or bored of participation sports, here are some spectator ones instead:

Powerboat Racing
End Nov–beginning Dec; www.f1h2o.com. The Class 1 World Powerboat Championship draws out local speedsters too, and concludes with a music festival of both local and international musicians.

UAE Football League
Sept–May weekday nights; various venues including Dubai and Abu Dhabi; www.uae football.org; fixtures: www.goalzz.com. Football fans will love the atmosphere and huge enthusiasm shown by teams and supporters.

SAILING AND KAYAKING

DUBAI

Dubai Offshore Sailing Club

Near KFC, Jumeira Road; tel: 04-394 1669; www.dosc.ae; daily 8am–9pm

This excellent RYA-approved, non-profit-making school offers courses, boat hire (including lasers and toppers), and a regular Friday race.

ABU DHABI

Noukhada Adventure Company

Tel: 02- 6503600; Meena Street; www.noukhada.ae; Mon–Sat 8.30am–5.30pm

Kayaking through the natural mangrove forests around Abu Dhabi is an unforgettable way to find peace in the city. Noukhada can also arrange catamaran sailing and cycling tours.

SCUBA-DIVING

An excellent source of information about diving in the UAE (including dive sites, centres, conditions, etc) is the Emirate Diving Association: www.emiratesdiving.com.

DUBAI

Al Boom Diving Club

Near Iranian Hospital, Corner of Al Wasl Road and 33rd Street; tel: 04-342 2993; www.alboom diving.com; Sat–Thur 9am–8pm, Fri 8am–7pm

A five-star-rated PADI dive school, Al Boom's offers courses including a four-day 'open water' for beginners, and daily diving and snorkelling trips off the coasts of Dubai, Fujairah and the Musandam peninsula, as well as a 'Shark Dive' in the Dubai Aquarium. Facilities include a pool, full equipment rental

Right: jetskis are available for hire in both cities.

and a well-stocked shop. Al Boom Diving Centres can also be found at Jebel Ali Dubai Golf Resort and Spa and at Atlantis the Palm.

ABU DHABI

Arabian Divers & Sport Fishing Charters

Al Bateen Marina, Al Bateen; tel: 050-614 6931; www.fishabu dhabi.com; Sat–Thur 8am–9pm, Fri 9am–4pm; map p.136 A2

One of the oldest diving and fishing outfits in Abu Dhabi, Arabian Divers offers snorkelling, diving and sightseeing boat tours, plus big game sportfishing. PADI dive courses are offered, and facilities include a training pool, classroom, retail shop and air filling stations.

SNOW SPORTS

DUBAI

Ski Dubai Snow Park

Mall of the Emirates, Sheikh Zayed Road; tel: 04-409 4000; www.skidxb.com; admission charge; Sun–Wed 10am–11pm, Thur 10am–midnight, Fri 9am–midnight, Sat 9am–11pm

Ski Dubai is one of the city's top attractions. Even if you've seen snow plenty of times before (unlike many locals), it's still fascinating for its novelty – skiing in the desert. On Monday, a DJ spices up the ski slopes.
SEE ALSO CHILDREN, P.41

KITESURFING

DUBAI

Kitesurfing Club

Kite Beach, behind Sunset Mall between Dubai Offshore Sailing Club and Jumeirah Beach Park; tel: 050-254 7440

Frenchman Xavier has set up the only kitesurfing club in the city. Call for details.

SURFING

Surf Dubai

Villa 12a, Street 3a, Beachside, Umm Suqueim 3; tel: 050-504 3020; www.surfingdubai.com; 7am–6.30pm

Dubai's first and only surf school, Surf Dubai, meet on Sunset Beach near the Burj Dubai whenever surf is forecasted. Check their website for the week's forecast, then call or email to book a lesson or board. Special beginners' boards are available.

WATER-SKIING AND WAKEBOARDING

DUBAI

Dubai Bristol Water Sport Academy

Dubai Marina, Marina Walk; tel: 04-366 3538; www.bristol-middleeast.com; Sun–Thur 10am–7pm

The French-run academy offers instructors and equipment for wakeboarding, wakesurfing and wakeskating, as well as kneeboarding and waterskiing. Speedboat trips, banana rides and doughnuts are also available for kids.

ABU DHABI

Beach Rotana Hotel

10th Street; tel: 02-697 9000; www.rotana.com/property-4.htm; daily 9am–6pm; map p.137 E2

The Rotana's beach club offers a good range of water sports with both instruction and equipment hire available, including all gear and boats for wakeboarding and water-skiing.

WIND/KITE SURFING

DUBAI

Kiting has been called the most exciting water sport on Earth. Conditions for kiting are good in Dubai, though the sport is subject to strict regulations.

North Kites

Al Bahar Showroom, Jumeira Road; tel: 04-394 1258; Sat–Thur 9am–9pm, Fri 4–9pm; admission charge

North Kites offers classes in the sport and advice on how to get started for both beginners and seasoned kiters.

ABU DHABI

Beach Rotana Hotel

10th Street; tel: 02-697 9000; www.rotana.com/property-4.htm; daily 8am–6pm; map p.139 E2

Offering an attractive, white stretch of beach, well-maintained equipment as well as good value for money, the Beach is a good choice for windsurfing.

Theatre, Dance, Music, Literature and Film

Dubai and Abu Dhabi are often dismissed as cultural vacuums. Worse, they're accused of committing the cardinal cultural sins of concreting over traditional culture in the rush to modernise, and importing in its place the most banal cultural imports from the West. While this is to quite a large degree true, grass-root-art movements, particularly in film and art, are beginning to stir.

THEATRE

While Dubai has no dedicated scene, it has passionate amateur thespians who perform with **Dubai Drama Group** (www.dubaidrama group.org) as well as varied productions at the theatres listed below.

Dubai Community Theatre & Arts Centre (DUCTAC)

Near Magic Planet, Level 2, Mall of the Emirates, Sheikh Zayed Road; tel: 04-341 4777 ext 314; www.ductac.org; Mon–Thur, Sat, Sun 9am–10pm, Fri 2–10pm; admission charge

The non-profit-making, community-rooted complex consists of two auditoriums and an exhibition space. Productions range from local student versions of modern classics, and Emirati displays of traditional dancing, to touring international troupes. DUCTAC also houses **The Old Library** (Sat–Thur 10am–6pm) which often hosts events of the Emirates Airline Festival of Literature.

Above: performer at Dubai International Jazz Festival.

Madinat Theatre

Madinat Jumeirah complex, Jumeira Road; tel: 04-366 6546; www.madinattheatre.com; opening hours vary; admission charge

Madinat stages a mixture of crowd-pulling mainstream drama and cabaret-style acts, plus children's entertainment. International musicals such as *Chicago* are increasingly coming to town here.

DANCE AND MUSIC

Your best chance to experience traditional Emirati dance and music is at the

Heritage & Diving Village in Dubai and the **Heritage Village** in Abu Dhabi, where displays are usually put on during festivals and holidays.
SEE ALSO MUSEUMS AND GALLERIES, P.84, 88

CONTEMPORARY

Modern music movements are still in their infancy, though some local groups are beginning to emerge.

Dubai International Jazz Festival

Dubai Media City, Al Sufouh Road, three days; www.dubai jazzfest.com

Though past headliners (such as Bee Gee Robin Gibb) have sparked controversy among purist jazz fans, the festival still attracts some of the world's best jazz performers. The jazz festival also takes place at Festival Park, Dubai Festival City.

LITERATURE

Extending back millennia, poetry was a highly valued skill in traditional Bedouin

Left, ballet at the Madinat Theatre.

society. Today, poetry is still revered, evidenced from student scribblings in magazines and newspapers, and the published musings of Sheikh Mohammed. Leading Emirati poets with books published in English include Sultan Al Owais.

Dubai now hosts its own literary festival: **Dubai's Emirates Airline International Festival of Literature** (late Feb–early Mar; Dubai Festival City; www.eaifl.com).

FILM

The history of Emirati cinema began with *Al Hilm* (the Dream) by Hani Al Shabani. Film is becoming a more important art form in the Emirates and 2009 saw feature film *City of Life* by Emirati Ali F. Mostafa push Dubai forward in its cinematic achievements. It's a very watchable film and a decent portrayal of the many lives and lifestyles that coexist in the cultural melting pot which is Dubai.

Facilities

Recent films shot in Dubai include George Clooney's *Syriana*, *The Alchemist*, *Code 46* and most recently *Mission Impossible 4* which featured Tom Cruise dangling off Burj Khalifa; Jamie Foxx's *The Kingdom* was filmed in Abu Dhabi.

In a bid to attract more Hollywood studios and talent, Dubai has constructed **Dubai Studio City** (www.dubaistudiocity.ae), equipped with world-class production technology. There were plans to build **Universal City** in Dubailand, which was going to contain among other things a Dubai outlet of the famous Universal Studios, as well as a 'ride the movies' theme park. However so far only a site for it has been found in the desert and it remains just one of the many projects planned for the city.

Festivals

Dubai's increasingly high-profile **International Film Festival** (www.dubaifilm fest.com; Dec; one week) premières films, documentaries and reasonably eclectic world and local features from India, Arab countries, Asia and the West. Its Muhr Award for Arab Cinema is considered a very prestigious prize.

Other film festivals include the annual principal **Abu Dhabi Film Festival** (www.abudhabifilmfestival. com).

CINEMAS

DUBAI

Megapix
Ibn Battuta Mall, Sheikh Zayed Road; tel: 04-366 9898; www.grandcinemas.com
The 21-screen Megaplex boasts good facilities including an IMAX screen.

ABU DHABI

Vox Cinema
Marina Mall, Breakwater; tel: 02-681 8484; www.uae.voxcinemas.com; map p.136 B3
The Vox is one the most modern and well-equipped cinemas in town. 'Vox Gold' service is also available.

SAADIYAT ISLAND

One day this island will be the home of Abu Dhabi's **Performing Arts Centre**. It's designed by Zaha Hadid and will be visually stunning inside and out. Visitors who wish to see the island firsthand as it changes and check out the ideas for the island's development can use the new Saadiyat Bridge. Head for the Manarat Al Saadiyat exhibition centre which hosts cultural and art exhibitions.

123

Transport

The Emirates are well served by transport, particularly air and road. The car is still king in both Dubai and Abu Dhabi, though both towns' municipalities are attempting little by little to remedy this dependency, most notably in the shape of Dubai's spanking-new metro system, increasing river transport on Dubai's Creek and developing the bus services in both cities. In the meantime, rush hour (7–9am, 1–2pm and 5–7pm) can paralyse the towns. Street identification can also be tricky, with roads called after their official names, nicknames and numbers. Most are identified by landmarks such as hotels, petrol stations or banks.

GETTING THERE

BY SEA

Boats (hydrofoil and dhow services) usually run between Dubai and several ports in Iran, and sometimes Iraq, taking between 12 and 48 hours, depending on the service and destination. Check the Dubai Ports Authority for further details: www.dpa.co.ae

BY ROAD

Oman borders the UAE to the north and east, Saudi Arabia to the south and west. Roads linking the three countries are good, but visas (notoriously prescriptive for Saudi Arabia), and passports are required. If driving, bring your driving licence and vehicle insurance documents which must cover you for both countries. Note that most rental companies in the UAE do not permit cross-border travel unless specifically arranged. You can contact the Road Traffic Authority on tel: 800 9090 (www.dubaipolice.gov.ae).

BY AIR

Airlines

Currently over 120 airlines fly to Dubai and Abu Dhabi serving nearly 200 destinations. Direct flights link Dubai or Abu Dhabi to most major European and Asian cities (plus several US and Australian hubs, including New York). As the airports and facilities of both cities expand, growing numbers of airlines stop over here (particularly Dubai with its 'open skies' policy) en route to Europe, Africa and Asia. For a list of airlines operating regular services, see: www.dubaiairport.com and www.abudhabiairport.ae

Air Fares

If you're looking for a cheaper air ticket to Dubai, it's worth checking out Etihad's competitive fares to Abu Dhabi; the airport is just half an hour by taxi from Dubai's Marina, and Etihad passengers are entitled to use the free shuttle bus that runs from Abu Dhabi airport to the Etihad offices in Dubai (tel: Chelsea Tower, Sheikh Zayed Road, Dubai; 04-343 4443; www.etihadair.com), though you'll need to book.

Airports

Facilities at Dubai and Abu Dhabi's excellent and ever-expanding airports include internet access, banking, restaurants, business services, hotels, bars, a golf course and the famous duty-free shopping, as well as raffles with good odds of winning cash prizes or luxury cars. To ease your passage from the plane, through immigration and into a taxi, you can pre-book for a reasonable fee the 'Marhaba Service' (www.marhabaservices.com). Most upper-rated hotels provide complimentary pick-up and drop-off services. Dubai international airport lies just 6km (4 miles) southeast of the city centre, Abu Dhabi's airport 22km (13 miles) from the city centre on the road leading northeast to Dubai.

Carbon calculators such as CarbonOrg (www.climate care.org) allow air travellers to offset their carbon footprint with a financial contribution to sustainable schemes worldwide that aim to reduce global warming.

GETTING AROUND

BUS

Most visitors use the cities' ubiquitous and relatively inexpensive taxi services. Buses, though extremely cheap and air-conditioned, are often infrequent and crowded, and the routes require acquaintance.

The two main local bus stations in Dubai are Deira bus station also known as Gold Souk Bus Station, and Bur Dubai bus station (p.130 B3) also known as Al Ghubaiba, and in Abu Dhabi on Hazza bin Zayed Road.

Buses run from around 6am–11pm. Route maps,

prices and timetables are available from the Road Transport Authority: www.rta.ae, as well as the cities' main bus terminals. Both cities are currently upping the number of buses, bus routes and bus shelters (air-conditioned) in a bid to quadruple the percentage of bus passengers (just 7 percent of the population currently). The excellent Emirates Express (running every 20 minutes peak times, every 40 minutes off-peak; daily 6am–9pm; two hours) run by the two cities' municipalities link Dubai and Abu Dhabi.

METRO

The much-anticipated, Japanese-built Dubai metro has transformed city travel for both the city's inhabitants and its visitors, the only problem being that even walking a short distance to a station is unbearable in the hot months. As part of the Dh15.8-billion megaproject, four lines (and multiple bullet-shaped stations) were planned: the Red, Green, Purple and Blue, as well as tram lines. The Red and Green lines opened in September 2009; the Green Line in March 2010; no date has been announced for the Purple or Blue lines.

The Red line, running for 52km (32 miles), connects, among other destinations, the airport (Terminals 1 and 3) to Deira and then travel along Sheikh Zayed Road to Jebel Ali. The 22km (13-mile) Green Line will connect Deira, Bur Dubai, the mouth of the Creek and Business Bay.

For timetables, prices and other information, see: www.rta.ae. There is an excellent download available on this site called Metro Pocket Brochure. There are various restrictions when using the metro including a limit on baggage allowed and fines are in place for those who break the rules, including chewing gum on a train. Trains run on average every 4 to 6 minutes. The Red line is more frequent than the Green. The driverless trains will accommodate 643 seated passengers and contain Gold, Silver and standard classes, as well as

The emirate of Dubai's airline is **Emirates** (www.emirates.com); that of Abu Dhabi (and the UAE's national airline) is **Etihad** (www.etihadair.com). Both have good safety records, though the once much-lauded service of Emirates has received fewer accolades recently. In 2007, the Kuwaiti airline **Al Jazeera** (www.jazeeraairways.com) became the first airline to fly to Dubai. Also worth checking for fares is **Air Arabia** (www.airarabia.com), the first low-cost airline in the Middle East, which is based in neighbouring emirate, Sharjah. The air travel high season is generally December to January and June to August.

Above: Dubai's official airline.

areas reserved for women and children, wheel chair users and elderly passengers. Metro facilities will include toilets, parking at the stations, bus stops and taxi stands, ticketing booths and vending machines. An e-friendly, credit-chargeable 'Contactless Smart Card' called a NOL card is good for all modes of public transport, including metro and bus, and allows travellers to switch seamlessly from one mode of transport to another through a unified fare. A red ticket NOL is generally the most convenient for visitors to Dubai.

TAXIS

Both cities boast good taxi services. Official taxis are metered, air-conditioned and comfortable, and most drivers have a basic (or better) command of English. There are Salik tolls (toll gates) on some routes and it will cost fractionally more to go through these. Sometimes a driver may ask if

you have a preferred route for this reason. There are few addresses in Dubai; street names and building numbers are rare. There are no postal deliveries to residences for this reason, It can make getting around difficult but if you can mention a nearby landmark to a taxi driver then you'll find yourself in the right vicinity at least.

Taxi stands are always found outside the major hotels and mall, though at peak times you can queue an hour or more at the latter. If visiting an attraction outside the city centre (such as at the Grand Mosque in Abu Dhabi), ask the cab that brought you to wait for you (metered rates are reasonable). During the rush hour it can be very difficult to find cabs in either city. There's also a dearth around the *abra* stations in Deira and by the bus station in Bur Dubai.

You can call a cab through **Dubai Transport** (tel: 04-339 0002) or **National Transport Company** (NTC; tel: 02-622 3300) in Abu Dhabi, though at rush hour it can be difficult to get through, or you may have to wait some time. Avoid unofficial cabs, and be aware

that the dedicated taxi services offered by many four- and five-star hotels are costlier. **Al Ghazal** (02-444 7787) in Abu Dhabi runs an efficient, reliable and competitively-priced Abu Dhabi–Dubai taxi service.

WATER TAXIS – ABRAS

Dubai's motorised *abras* (water taxis) ferry the city's thousands of commuters back and forth across the Creek. Operating from 5am to midnight daily, they are a great way of crossing the Creek, particularly during the road rush hour. A trip also makes a dirt-cheap (albeit short) river ride, though you can also charter one just for yourself.

There are three main *abra* routes. Bur Dubai Abra Station (map p.130 B2) to Deira Old Souk Abra Station (map p.130 B2), Al Seef Station (map p.130 B2) to Baniyas Station (map p.130 C2) in Deira, and from Dubai Old Souk Abra Station (map p.130 B2) to Sabkha Abra Station (map p.130 C2).

WATERBUSES

More comfortable than the *abras*, and air-conditioned (essential in summer), are Dubai's waterbuses, which run from 6am to 11pm daily along five main routes: from Bur Dubai Abra Station (map p.130 B2) to Sabkha Abra Station (map p.130 B2); from Al Seef (map p.130 C2) to Sabka Station (map p.130 C2) via Baniyas Station; from Baniyas Station to Dubai Old Souk (map p.130 B2); from Dubai Old Souk to Sakkha Station; and a 'tourist line' from Al Shindagha Station to Al Seef Station and vice versa. In mid-2009, Dubai's Roads & Transport Authority decided to bring the price down to just Dh4 for a round trip, in a bid to encourage people off the roads.

CAR HIRE

Car-hire companies can be found in the Arrivals hall of both cities' airports (many of them open 24 hours), as well as at the cities' main hotels. To rent a car, drivers must be over 21; over 25 to rent a medium (2 litre or above) vehicle or 4WD. Most national driving licences are accepted by most companies, third-party insurance is obligatory, and you'll need a credit card for the deposit.

There are 24-hour petrol stations on all the major roads, and both free and pay parking in many places. Roads are well marked, with signs in both English and Arabic. Petrol is cheap. When hiring a car (particularly from a small outfit) do check the cars are fitted with Salik cards which allow the car to drive through a number of tolls. Otherwise the car

may be fined whenever it goes through the toll and the fine may be passed on to the driver at the time.

Road Rules

Driving is on the right, front seatbelts are compulsory (and rear seatbelts are strongly advised), and use of handheld mobile phones whilst driving is illegal. Children under 10 years old must sit in the back of the car.

Speed Limits

Speed limits are the following: 40kph (25mph) in residential areas (though it can be up to 80kph/50mph), 100kph (60mph) on the city highways and 120kph (75mph) outside the cities.

Local Driving

Many road rules and protocol (such as proper use of indicators, mirrors, lanes and minimum distance-maintaining) are ignored by local drivers. Drive cautiously and defensively, particularly along the 'super highways' with up to 10 lanes, and look out in particular for drivers lane-hopping, pulling out suddenly, swerving, speeding, tail-gaiting and driving too aggressively.

Alcohol

Note that both Dubai and Abu Dhabi's police operate a strict zero-tolerance policy on drinking and driving. Random spot checks are increasing, and penalties, particularly if involved in an accident whether serious or not and whether your fault or not, are severe, including heavy fines and prison.

Road Incidents

Road accidents in Dubai and Abu Dhabi are among the highest per capita in the world, due to rule-breaking, speeding and inexperienced drivers. There is a fatality in the cities every 24 hours, an accident every two. If you have a serious accident, call 999; if minor: 04-398 1111 in Dubai, 02-681 2200 in Abu Dhabi.

Note that if driving a rented car, you must report all damage to police, otherwise the hired car's insurers will not cover it (and you will have to instead). If there is uncertainty regarding whose fault the accident was, or someone is injured, leave the cars where they are until the police arrive. If you break down, call the Arabian Automobile Association free on: 000-4000 (www.aaauae.com).

Right: Chevy's first hybrid vehicle goes on show in Dubai.

Atlas

The following streetplans of Dubai and Abu Dhabi make it easy to find the attractions listed in our A–Z section. A selective index to streets and sights will help you find other locations throughout the cities.

Map Legend

▮ Notable building		❶	Tourist information
▮ Souk / market / mall		★	Sight of interest
▮ Transport hub		Ⓜ	Metro station
▮ Hotel		⛴	Abra station
▮ Park		🚌	Bus station
▮ Beach		☪	Mosque
▮ Urban area		✡	Synagogue
▮ Non-urban area		✚	Cathedral / church
)····(Tunnel		✉	Post office
✝ ✧ Cemetery		📖	Library
		✚	Hospital
		👤	Statue / monument

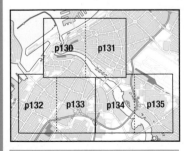

Abu Dhabi	p136 – 137
Dubai Metro system	p138

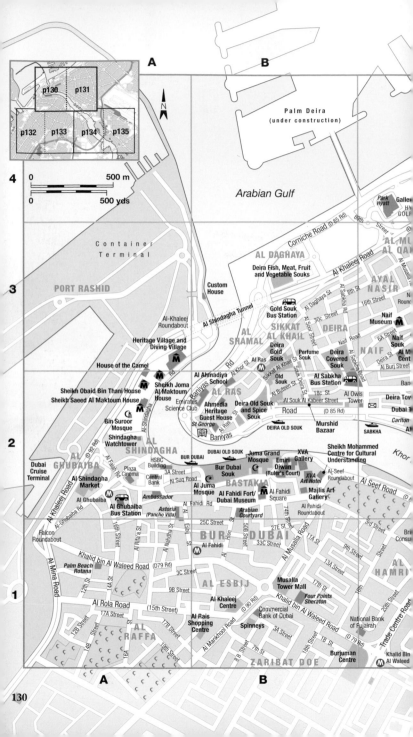

A

B

p130 p131

p132 p133 p134 p135

N

4

0   500 m

0   500 yds

Arabian Gulf

Palm Deira
(under construction)

Container
Terminal

PORT RASHID

Park
Hyatt

Galler
HY
GOLF

3

Corniche Road (D 85 Rd)

69th
Street

89th
Street

**AL MU
AL QA**

Custom
House

Al-Khaleej
Roundabout

Al Shindagha Tunnel

AL DAGHAYA

**Deira Fish, Meat, Fruit
and Vegetable Souks**

Al Khaleej Road

Al Musalla

**AYAL
NASIR**

16th Street

Round

Gold Souk
Bus Station

**SIKKAT
AL KHAIL**

Al Daghaya St

Al Sabkha Rd

Al 8th St

30C Street

6A Street

DEIRA

Naif
Museum

NAIF

Naif
Souk

Naif M
Cent

Heritage Village and
Diving Village

**AL
SHAMAL**

AL RAS

Baniyas Rd

Al Ras

Al Khor St

**Deira
Gold
Souk**

**Perfume
Souk**

**Deira
Covered
Souk**

Al Khail St

Deira St

Al Burj Street

Deira Tow

House of the Camel

**Al Ahmadiya
School**

Sheikh Joma
Al Maktoum
House

Sheikh Obaid Bin Thani House

Sheikh Saeed Al Maktoum House

Emirates
Science Club

**Ahmedia
Heritage
Guest House**

St George

Baniyas
Al Ras

**Old
Souk**

Al Buteen St

18c. St

**Deira Old Souk
and Spice
Souk**

Al Souk Al Kabeer Street

Road   (D 85 Rd)

DEIRA OLD SOUK

Al Owis
Tower

Deira Tow

Dubai T

Carlton

SABKHA

AM

**Al Sabkha
Bus Station**

Murshid
Bazaar

Bin Suroor
Mosque

Shindagha
Watchtower

**AL
SHINDAGHA**

Al-Shindagha

Al Ras Rd

Al Falah Rd

Plaza
Cinema

HSBC
Building

Central
Bank

3A Street

Al Suq Road

BUR DUBAI

DUBAI OLD SOUK

Bur Dubai
Souk

**Juma Grand
Mosque**

Emiri
Diwan
(Ruler's Court)

**XVA
Gallery**

**Sheikh Mohammed
Centre for Cultural
Understanding**

Khor

2

**AL
GHUBAIBA**

Dubai
Cruise
Terminal

Al Ghubaiba Rd

Al Khaleej Road

**Al Shindagha
Market**

Al Ghubaiba

**Al Ghubaiba
Bus Station**

Ambassador

Astoria
(Pancho Villa)

**Al Juma
Mosque**

Al Fahidi Rd

BASTAKIA

Al Fahidi Fort/
Dubai Museum

Al Fahidi
Square

**XVA
Art Hotel**

**Majlis Art
Gallery**

Al-Seef
Roundabout

Al Fahidi
Roundabout

Al Seef Road

(D

3rd Street

Falcon
Roundabout

Al Mina Road

Khalid bin Al Waleed Road

(D79 Rd)

16th Street

Al Rifa St

Al Nandha St

Eslid

25C Street

**Arabian
Courtyard**

Al Fahidi

**BUR
DUBAI**

508 Street

27E St

33C Street

Al Musalla Road

17A St

9th Street

13A Street

Bri
Consu

**AL
HAMRI**

Palm Beach
Rotana

12th St

14A St

(15th Street)

3C Street

9B Street

AL ESBIJ

Musalla
Tower Mall

17th St

Khalid bin Al Waleed Road

**Four Points
Sheraton**

1

Al Rola Road

17A Street

12B Street

14A Street

**AL
RAFFA**

17B Street

18th Street

**Al Khaleej
Centre**

**Al Rais
Shopping
Centre**

Al Mankhool Road

(D 90 Rd)

Spinneys

7th Street

3A Street

8 B Street

Commercial
Bank of Dubai

Khalid bin Al Waleed Road

(D 79 Rd)

18th Street

1 B St

National Bank
of Fujairah

20th Street

Khalid Bin
Al Waleed

**Burjuman
Centre**

ZARIBAT DOE

Trade Centre Road

A

B

A

B

p130 p131
p132 p133 p134 p135

4

Arabian Gulf

Dubai Dry Dock

Department of Ports and Customs

Port Administration

Seaview

AL MINA

AL RAFFA

17A Street

123 Street

14B Street

16 St

16A Street

Kuwait Road (D 92 Rd)

Al Mina Road (D 92 Rd)

Dubai International Seafarers Centre

(D 77 Rd)

Dhow Palace Hotel

Chelsea

Al Adhid Road (D 75 Rd)

(D 90 Rd)

23A Street

25A Street

3

4th Street

Dubai Port Police Headquarters

4th Street

Al Mina Road (D 92 Rd)

4th Street

1st Street

5th Street

8A St

Al Mankhool Road

2B Street

32A Street

4E Street

AL MANKHOOL

35A Street

43A Street

12C Street

33rd

Al Qataiyat Road (D 75 Rd)

Mussallah Al Eid

3rd Street

Umer Ibn Al Khattab Mosque ★

7th Street

2B Street

1B Street

9th Street

11th Street

38A Street

Al Dhiyafa Roundabout

AL HUDHEIBA

21st Street

4B

6B

15th Street

8C

23A Street

13A Street

31A Street

34th Street

36th Street

42nd Street

AL JAFILYA

39B Street

2

10A Street

16A Street

3rd Street

5B Street

30B Street

Al Wasl Road (D 92 Rd)

2A Street

7A Street

9th St

6A Street

8A Street

12A

14A Street

20A Street

Al Dhiyafah Road

Jumeira Rotana

Dune Centre

Al Satwa Roundabout

Al Hana Centre

35th Street

39A St

6C Street

12B Street

16th Street

22nd Street

31B Street

45B Street

39B Street

29C St

Department Health and Med Ser

Al Ja

Passport and Immigration Office

Trade Centre (

✉ **Al Satwa**

Al Dhiyafah Road

9th Street

(D 73 Rd)

Public Arts Association

Bur Dubai Police Station

55B Street

67C Street

28th Street

32nd Street

47B St

47B St

1

6B St

Al Hudheiba Road

21st Street

Satwa Souk

Al Satwa Road (D 90 Rd)

17th Street

19th Street

10B Street

Satwa Souk

13th Street

3rd Street

AL BADA'A

N

12B St

4th Street

Satwa Souk

21st Street

22A Street

30A

AL SATWA

Sheikh Zayed Road (E 11 Rd)

30B Street

Fairmont Dubai

H Hotel

Za'abeel Roundabout

Dubai World Trade Centre

Ⓜ World Trade Centre

Ibis WTC

2nd Za'abeel Road

Dubai International Conference Centre

API World Tower

0 —— 500 m

0 —— 500 yds

132

A

B

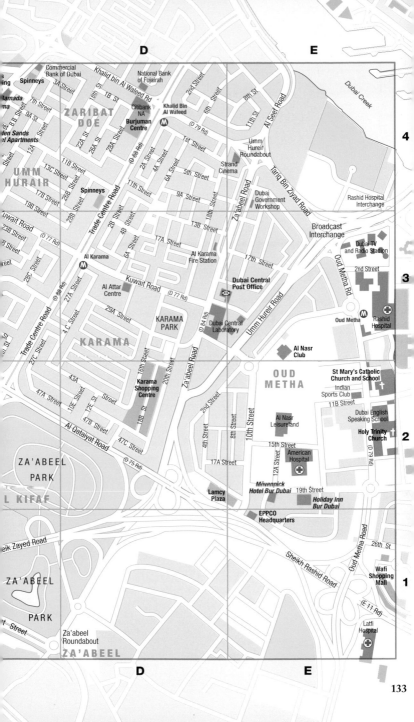

D

E

Commercial Bank of Dubai

National Bank of Fujairah

Spinneys

Khalid bin Al Waleed Rd

ing

Spinneys

7th Street

3A Street

18th

1B St

2nd Street

6th Street

8th St

Al Seef Road

Dubai Creek

4

amada
na

9A St

8 B Street

Citibank NA

Khalid Bin Al Waleed

11th St

ZARIBAT DOE

Burjuman Centre

(D 79 Rd)

en Sands
el Apartments

12A

22A St

26A St

28A Street

2A Street

4A Street

1st Street

Umm Hureir Roundabout

reet

UMM HURAIR

11B Street

13C Street

28D Street

11th Street

5th Street

6A Street

9A Street

Tariq Bin Ziyad Road

uwait Road

Trade Centre Road

2B Street

T3B Street

18th Street

Za'abeel Road

Strand Cinema

Dubai Government Workshop

Rashid Hospital Interchange

17B Street

19B Street

29B Street

4B Street

17A Street

Al Karama Fire Station

Broadcast Interchange

23B Street

(D 77 Rd)

Kuwait Road

Al Karama

6A Street

17th Street

Dubai TV and Radio Station

Oud Metha Rd

2nd Street

B Street

reet

Al Attar Centre

27A Street

(D 78 Rd)

29A Street

Kuwait Road

(D 77 Rd)

Dubai Central Post Office

Umm Hureir Road

Oud Metha

Rashid Hospital

3

20B Street

Trade Centre Road

4 C Street

KARAMA PARK

Dubai Central Laboratory

KARAMA

Al Nasr Club

27C Street

16th Street

20th Street

Za'abeel Road

OUD METHA

St Mary's Catholic Church and School

43A

11E Street

12E St

Karama Shopping Centre

13B St

2nd Street

8th Street

10th Street

Indian Sports Club

11B Street

47A Street

47B Street

18B St

Al Nasr Leisureland

Dubai English Speaking School

ZA'ABEEL PARK

Al Qataiyat Road

47C Street

(D 75 Rd)

4th Street

8th Street

15th Street

12A Street

American Hospital

Holy Trinity Church

(D 79 Rd)

2

17A Street

Lamcy Plaza

Mövennick Hotel Bur Dubai

19th Street

Holiday Inn Bur Dubai

L KIFAF

EPPCO Headquarters

eik Zayed Road

Sheikh Rashid Road

Oud Metha Road

26th St

ZA'ABEEL PARK

t Street

Za'abeel Roundabout

Sheik Zayed Road

Wafi Shopping Mall

1

(E 11 Rd)

Latfi Hospital

ZA'ABEEL

D

E

133

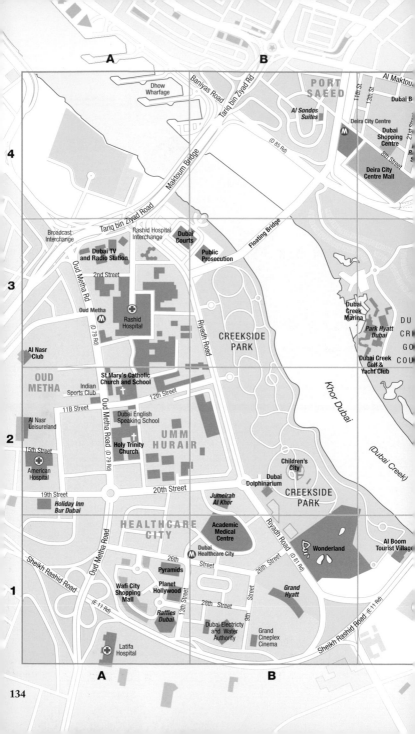

A   **B**

Dhow Wharfage

Banjyas Road

Tariq bin Ziyad Rd

PORT SAEED

11th St.

13th St.

Dubai B

Al Sondos Suites

Deira City Centre

21st St.

Dubai Shopping Centre

(D 85 Rd)

8th Street

4

Maktoum Bridge

Deira City Centre Mall

R
S

Tariq bin Ziyad Road

Broadcast Interchange

Rashid Hospital Interchange

Dubai Courts

Floating Bridge

Dubai TV and Radio Station

Public Prosecution

Oud Metha Rd

2nd Street

(D 79 Rd)

Dubai Creek Marina

Park Hyatt Dubai

DU
CR
GO
COU

3

Oud Metha

Rashid Hospital

CREEKSIDE PARK

Dubai Creek Golf & Yacht Club

Al Nasr Club

OUD METHA

St Mary's Catholic Church and School

Khor Dubai

Indian Sports Club

12th Street

11B Street

Dubai English Speaking School

UMM HURAIR

Al Nasr Leisureland

Oud Metha Road (D 79 Rd)

Holy Trinity Church

(Dubai Creek)

2

15th Street

Children's City

American Hospital

20th Street

Dubai Dolphinarium

CREEKSIDE PARK

19th Street

Jumeirah Al Khor

Holiday Inn Bur Dubai

Riyadh Road

Sheikh Rashid Road

HEALTHCARE CITY

Academic Medical Centre

Riyadh Road (D 81 Rd)

Wonderland

Al Boom Tourist Village

Oud Metha Road

Dubai Healthcare City

26th Street

26th Street

Pyramids

9th Street

Grand Hyatt

1

Wafi City Shopping Mall

Planet Hollywood

13th Street

28th Street

Street

Sheikh Rashid Road (E 11 Rd)

(E 11 Rd)

Raffles Dubai

Dubai Electricity and Water Authority

Grand Cineplex Cinema

Latifa Hospital

A   **B**

134

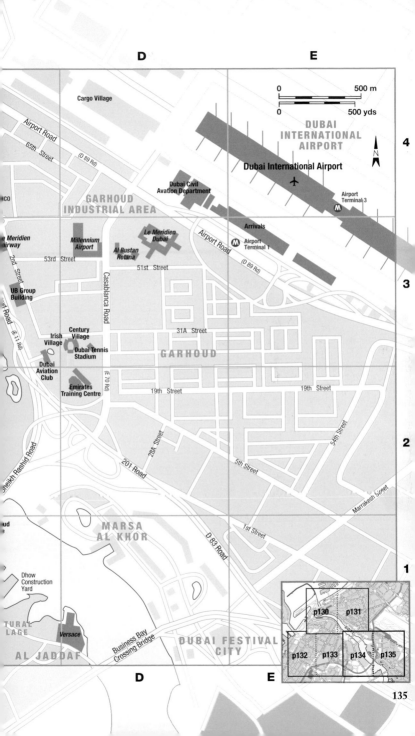

D   **E**

0 _____ 500 m
0 _____ 500 yds

Cargo Village

Airport Road

65th Street

(D 89 Rd)

**DUBAI
INTERNATIONAL
AIRPORT**

N

4

Dubai International Airport

✈

NCO

**GARHOUD
INDUSTRIAL AREA**

Dubai Civil
Aviation Department

Airport
Terminal 3

Ⓜ

e Meridien
airway

Millennium
Airport

Le Meridien
Dubai

Airport Road

Arrivals

Airport
Terminal 1

Ⓜ

2nd Street

53rd Street

Al Bustan
Rotana

51st Street

(D 89 Rd)

3

UB Group
Building

Casablanca Road

Road

(E 11 Rd)

Irish
Village

Century
Village

31A Street

GARHOUD

Dubai Tennis
Stadium

Dubai
Aviation
Club

(E 70 Rd)

Emirates
Training Centre

19th Street

19th Street

54th Street

2

Sheikh Rashid Road

29A Street

201 Road

5th Street

Marrakesh Street

**MARSA
AL KHOR**

D 83 Road

1st Street

1

Dhow
Construction
Yard

TURAL
LAGE

ud

Versace

AL JADDAF

Business Bay
Crossing Bridge

**DUBAI FESTIVAL
CITY**

p130 p131
p132 p133 p134 p135

D   **E**

ABU DHABI

A   B

4

Arabian Gulf

MARINA

★ Heritage Village

Marina Mall

Abu Dhabi International Sailing School

Abu Dhabi Theater ★

3

Ladies' Beach

AL RAS AL AKHDAR

Abu Dhabi Ladies' Club

Public Beach

18th Street

BREAKWATER

★ Flag
★ Heritage Village

WEST CORNICHE

Emirates Palace

Hiltonia Beach Club

Corniche West

Presidential Palace

Corniche Road West

AL MARKAZ GARD

Street

Jumerah at Emirates Towers

Hilton International Abu Dhabi

AL KHUBEIRAH PARK

6th St

AL KHALIDIYA

5th St

ZALAMAT GARDEN

KHALIDIYAH LADIES PARK

Al Bateen Dhow Building Yard ★

34th Street

AL KHUDEIRAH

Sheikh Zayed the First Street

KHALIDIYAH GARDEN

Khalidiyah Ma

2

COCONUT ISLAND

InterContinental

13th Street

Sultan Bin Zayed Street

4th St

19th Street

AL BATEEN

Al Manhal Stre

16th Street

Marina

9th St

Bainunah Street

Al Khaleeg Al Arabi Street

Dhow Building Yard

Marina

Municipal Market

Al Bateen Market

CEMETERY

Khalifa Bin

Al Batin Street

1

Hideriyyat

Khor Al Bateen

AL BATEEN

10th St

32nd St

Al Khaleeg Al Arabi Street

Shakhbut Street

AL ROWD

Delma

0   1500 m

0   1500 yds

Al Bateen Palac

A   B

136

ABU DHABI

D **E**

4

Iranian Market

AL MEENA

Meena Centre

AL LULU

Lulu Island

Al Dafra Restaurant

DHOW HARBOUR

★ Dhow Cruise

Iranian Souk

EAST CORNICHE

Al Meena Fish Souk

Al Meena Fruit & Vegetable Souk

CORNICHE GARDENS

HERITAGE PARK

Carpet Souk

3

Corniche Road East

LAKE PARK

Corniche Rd East

FORMAL PARK
1st St

Liwa

Lulu

Umm

Al Nar Street

Le Royal Méridien

Sheraton Abu Dhabi Resort & Towers

Al Meena Street

12th St

AL MEENA

Corniche Road West

Khaleej Bin Al Waleed St

URBAN PARK

5th St

Souk

World Trade Center Central Market

Al Maha Rotana

Liwa Street

Sheikh Khalifa Bin Zayed

CAPITAL GARDEN

Grand Continental Flamingo

International Rotana

10th

Al Diar Regency

LY

asr St

Al Hosn Palace

Sheikh Hamdan Bin Mohammad Street

Liwa Centre

Hamdan Centre

Crowne Plaza

Umm Al Nar St

Hazza Bin Zayed Mosque

☪

2nd Street

Street

Le Méridien

Khor Laffan

ELCOTDA PARK

AL HOSN

Sheikh Zayed the Second Street

Al Salam Street

★ Abu Dhabi Marina and Yacht Club

Sheik Zayed II Mosque

☪

Madinat Zayed Shopping Centre

Sands

9th St

13th St

10th Street

Abu Dhabi Mall

Street

As Suwwah Island

2

Street

MANHAL

East Road

Gold Souk

MADINAT ZAYED

TOURIST CLUB AREA

Beach Rotana Hotel and Towers

Al Karamah

Manhal Place

Bani Yas

10th Street

19th St

ENTRAL

Sheikh Rashid Bin Saeed Al Maktoum Street

ABU

DHABI

Al Falah Street

AL DHAFRAH

Marina Square

SHEIKH KHALIFA MEDICAL CITY

(Old Airport Road)

Mushayarib Island

1

Street

Hazaa Bin Zayed Street

(Defence Road)

11th St

an

Street

Al Wahdah Mall

Grand Millennium Al Wahdah

🚗

AL WAHDAH

East Road

QASR EL BAHR

Khor Al Baghal

KARAMAH

Delma Street

Eastern Ring Road

AL MUSALLA

D **E**

137

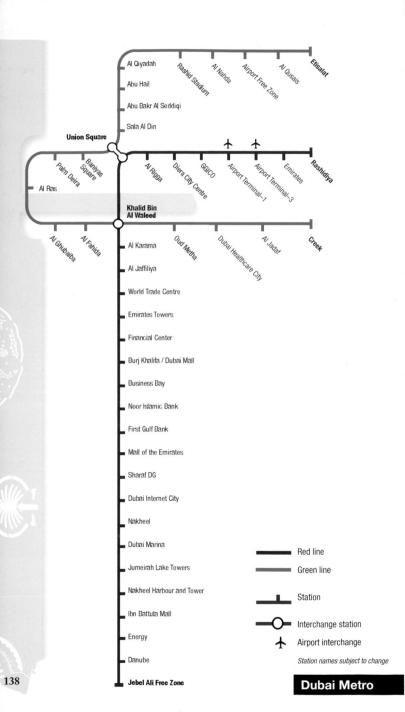

Al Qiyadah
Rashid Stadium
Al Nahda
Airport Free Zone
Al Qusais
Etisalat

Abu Hail

Abu Bakr Al Seddiqi

Sala Al Din

Union Square

Palm Deira
Baniyas Square

Al Rigga
Diera City Centre
GGICO
Airport Terminal–1
Airport Terminal–3
Emirates
Rashidiya

Al Ras

Khalid Bin Al Waleed

Al Ghubaiba
Al Fahidi

Oud Metha
Dubai Healthcare City
Al Jadaf
Creek

Al Karama

Al Jaffiliya

World Trade Centre

Emirates Towers

Financial Center

Burj Khalifa / Dubai Mall

Business Bay

Noor Islamic Bank

First Gulf Bank

Mall of the Emirates

Sharaf DG

Dubai Internet City

Nakheel

Dubai Marina

Jumeirah Lake Towers

Nakheel Harbour and Tower

Ibn Battuta Mall

Energy

Danube

Jebel Ali Free Zone

Red line

Green line

Station

Interchange station

Airport interchange

Station names subject to change

138

Dubai Metro

Dubai Atlas Index

Abu Dhabi Atlas Index

Index

143

Insight Smart Guide: Dubai and Abu Dhabi
Written by: Frances Linzee Gordon
Updated by: Caroline Alexander
Photography by: APA Matt Jones: 8, 15, 17B/T, 44, 46TR, 47B, 53, 58, 84B, 85BL, 89T; APA Chris Bradley 19, 21, 48/49, 62/63, 65l, 114/115; APA John Ishi 104; APA Kevin Cummins 6, 52B, 55, 56/57, 57B, 59R, 63B, 65M, 117L, 118/119; APA Glyn Genin 92T; ADTA 21, 46/47, 64T; Al Noofrah 107; Alamy 28/29, 30/31, 38, 52/53; Atlantis Hotels 40/41, 79, 108B; Bigstock 60B; Burj Al Arab 2/3, 11; Burj Jumeira 10, 71R; Corbis 54B, 60/61, 67MR, 84/85, 93T, 127; Dreamstime 7, 9, 26/27, 27, 67BR, 86, 98/99, 99B, 122C; Dubai Tourist Board 65R; Emirates Towers 77L, 77R, 96B; Fotolia 44/45; Getty 50/51, 51B, 67TL, 89B, 100T; Istockphoto 2B, 12, 14, 26T&B, 28B, 35T, 45B, 50B, 67BL, 82/83, 116; Jumeirah International LLC 74, 75, 90B, 93B, 112/113; Leonardo 3B, 70, 73, 76; Mary Evans Picture Library 66; Meridian Hotels 68/69, 80, 94/95, 102/103; Millennium Hotels 111; Paul Thuysbaert 30B 43B; Raffles Hotels 55B, 72, 114B, 124/125, 125B; Shangri La Hotels 78, 81; The Third Line Gallery 88; Wild Wadi 41B, 42; Yas Marina Circuit 23T
Second Edition 2013
© 2013 Apa Publications (UK) Limited
Printed by CTPS-China
Worldwide distribution enquiries:

APA Publications GmbH & Co Verlag KG (Singapore branch); 7030 Ang Mo Kio Ave 5, 08-65 Northstar @ AMK, Singapore 569880; email: apasin@singnet.com.sg
Distributed in the UK and Ireland by:
Dorling Kindersley Ltd (a Penguin Company); 80 Strand, London, WC2R 0RL, UK; email: customerservice@uk.dk.com
Distributed in the United States by:
Ingram Publisher Services
One Ingram Blvd, PO Box 3006, La Vergne, TN 37086-1986; email: customer.service@ingrampublisherservices.com
Distributed in Australia by:
Universal Publishers; PO Box 307, St. Leonards, NSW 1590; email: sales@universalpublishers.com.au
Distributed in New Zealand by:
Brown Knows Publications; 11 Artesia Close, Shamrock Park, Auckland, New Zealand 2016; email: sales@brownknows.co.nz
Contacting the Editors
We would appreciate it if readers would alert us to errors or outdated information by writing to: Apa Publications, PO Box 7910, London SE1 1WE, UK; fax: (44 20) 7403 0290; email: insight@apaguide.co.uk
No part of this book may be reproduced, stored in a retrieval system or transmitted in any form or by any means (electronic, mechanical, photocopying, recording or otherwise), without prior written permission of Apa Publications. Brief text quotations with use of photographs are exempted for book review purposes only. Information has been obtained from sources believed to be reliable, but its accuracy and completeness, and the

opinions based thereon, are not guaranteed.
Author Bio: Frances has travelled in nearly 100 countries of which the nations of the Middle East hold a special fascination. She has contributed guidebooks, features and photographs to a wide variety of international publications, as well as presenting, producing and consulting for television and radio including a recent BBC documentary on the ancient incense trail.
Author Thanks: Of the countless individuals who showed me the region's legendary kindness and hospitality, I would like to thank particularly the following: at the Department of Tourism & Commerce Marketing, Mr Saad El Sayed, Head of Arabic & English Media, Fatma Ahmed Yousif Al Hammadi, Senior Executive, and particularly Fatma Yousef Salem, Head of Research & Information who patiently responded to interminable questions, queries and requests; Mr Mohammed Alaoui , of Emirates Palace; Lisa Carusone, Jumeirah Group, for excellent tours of the Jumeirah properties; and Mr Darren Brews of Seawings. Special thanks to Danielle Aychouh at Towers Rotana; Maricel Gonzalez and Helena Al Sayed at Al Bustan Rotana for a warm welcome and great help with research; Moza Obaid Rashed at the GIS Center who patiently bore my supplications for maps, and to all at Dubai metro for generously providing unpublished blue prints. Thanks to Haroon Sugich of Trans-Arabian Creative Communications, who provided penetrating, original and stimulating insights into the region's politics. It was a pleasure to work with all. I dedicate this book to Domini Deitch, an unfailing friend for 20 years.